# IF YOU CAN'T CASHFLOW AFTER THIS

# IF YOU CAN'T CASHFLOW AFTER THIS

## I'VE GOT NOTHING FOR YOU...

Todd M Fleming

© 2018 Todd M Fleming
All rights reserved.

ISBN 13: 978-0-578-43247-2

# Table of Contents

Introduction: Continuing My Story ............................................. 1
My Story Continued ............................................................. 3
How Life Changes for the Better After Deal One ............................ 7
Money Story ..................................................................... 11
Pond Mentality .................................................................. 14
Why Checks Just Don't Work .................................................. 16
Building Credibility in Yourself ............................................... 19
How to Shift Perspective ....................................................... 22
Creating Money Out of Thin Air ............................................... 27
How to Eliminate Trading Time for Income to Set Yourself Free ........... 30
An Intro to Understanding How to Earn Money Passively ................... 34
Using Promissory Notes to Build Wealth ..................................... 38
The Pros of Owning Promissory Notes ....................................... 42
The Cons of Owning Promissory Notes ....................................... 46
Owning Rental Property and Sending Families to Work for You ........... 49
The Upside to Owning Rental Property ....................................... 51
The Downside to Owning Rental Property .................................... 56
The "Real Life Cell" on a Spreadsheet is Missing ............................ 59
Getting Clarity on Long-Term Financial Freedom ............................ 71
Assigning New Income to a Debt to Make it Free ............................ 74
Scaling and Team Building ..................................................... 77
Wholesaling for Truly Passive Income ........................................ 88

Case Studies .................................................................................... 94
    The Hoarder Home ................................................................... 95
    The Smoker Lounge ................................................................. 98

Step One ........................................................................................ 100
    Organizing Note/Title Company .............................................. 100
    Explaining Your Goals and Path ............................................... 102
    Understanding the Process ....................................................... 104

Step Two ........................................................................................ 110
    Locating Property at Discount by Locating Larger
    Problems to Solve .................................................................... 110
    What to Look for ..................................................................... 114
    Understanding Problem-Solving .............................................. 119
    What to Say and What Questions to Ask ................................. 123
    Understanding Sellers Don't Want Money ............................... 126
    How to Pair a Solution to Any Problem .................................. 128

Step Three ...................................................................................... 130
    What Can I Pay for This Property? .......................................... 130
    Exit Strategies .......................................................................... 134
    Wholesale ................................................................................. 136
    Wholetale ................................................................................. 138
    Retail Paper/Owning Debt ...................................................... 141
    Should I Rehab This Myself? ................................................... 145
    Rental Property ........................................................................ 148

Step Four ....................................................................................... 153
    Ranking the Exit Strategies to Choose Best Possible Offer ...... 153
    Putting the Offer on the Table ................................................ 158
    Ask Them How You Can Best Serve ....................................... 161

Explaining the Problem-Solving Process ............................................. 163

Step Five ................................................................................................. 165
    Accepted Offer Next Action Steps ..................................................... 165
    Can I Create Monthly Income for Free? ........................................... 167
    Do I Need to Gather More Resources? .............................................. 169
    Setting Expectations with Title Company or Attorney .................. 170
    Understand Your Security and Lien Position .................................. 171
    Closing Day ............................................................................................ 173

Step Six .................................................................................................. 176
    What to Expect After Closing ............................................................. 176
    Building an Intake System for the Business .................................... 181
    Your First Check and How to Expect to Feel ................................. 187
    How to Get it Again ............................................................................. 189
    What to Expect When Scaling ........................................................... 191
    Understanding Asset Classes .............................................................. 193

BONUS STEP: ..................................................................................... 196
    What if You Focus on Problems with Much Larger
    Properties Attached to Them? ............................................................ 196

Can I Receive Bulk Payments AND Passive Payments
from the Same Deal? ............................................................................ 199
Advantages of Leveraging Other Teams ................................................. 202
How to Obtain Equity in a Deal You Never Saw ................................. 204
You Can Do This on More Than Just Houses ...................................... 206
Mobile Home Case Study ......................................................................... 208
Closing Thoughts ....................................................................................... 211
Special Thanks ............................................................................................ 213
About the Author ...................................................................................... 216

Want to Work with Todd? .................................................. 217
Recommended Media ...................................................... 218
Todd's Other Books ........................................................ 219
Acknowledgements and Testimonials ................................. 220

*This Book Is For:*
*Those willing to accept delayed gratification and take the less comfortable path*

*Editing by:* Marianne Plunkert

*Cover Art by:* Kiel Fleming

# Introduction: Continuing My Story

In the first book of my "I've Got Nothing For You" series (*If You Can't Wholesale After This, I've Got Nothing For You*), you learned about my early attempts at business. I described the frustration, anger, fear, and depression I felt as I worked at an unfulfilling job within a cubicle for 40-plus hours a week while watching my dreams and energy slip away. I was gasping for freedom and opportunity. I wanted to feel like I was making an impact. I wanted to fulfill the expectations I had established for myself for the past two decades. Instead, I was 25 and miserable.

I know many of you may still relate to this feeling. I know how hard it can be to adjust and rise above fear. In my first book, you also learned that my first attempts in business didn't go as planned. I discovered the myth of the "overnight success." I learned how much hard work it really takes merely to survive in business, let alone thrive within it!

At the conclusion of my first book, I was just learning about wholesaling real estate and how to solve problems for sellers of property by connecting them with my network of performing buyers. My story continues in this book, and you will learn how I closed my first few deals, made my first $7,000, and eventually transitioned to generating multiple lines of repeat income with virtually zero risk and no upfront capital. You will also find that the first book's theme of asking great questions is maintained throughout this second installment. My belief in asking great questions and its direct correlation to your ability to advance your life is stronger than ever, and I want you to start injecting these questions into your business and personal life today! Not tomorrow. Today! I have moved from being completely dead broke, wondering where my next meal was going to come from, to living life on my terms, spending my days with my family, and building multiple businesses. I have come to realize that all of this was simply a choice. I had a choice to conform and stay where there was perceived security and safety, or I could choose to ask myself what my ideal day looked like and work towards that. Thankfully, I chose the latter and began working towards living the life that I had created in my mind.

**GREAT QUESTION: DO I CHOOSE TO LIVE MY LIFE AS I SEE FIT, OR DO I CHOOSE TO LIVE MY LIFE AS SOMEONE ELSE SEES FIT?**

# My Story Continued

*Today is the day!* I thought to myself. It was the morning of my first-ever closing. My first deal. My first real taste of success in real estate. I had successfully located a seller with a problem who I could pair with a buyer who wanted the property at a price on which we all agreed. This was the single most gratifying feeling I had ever experienced. This was better than playing college baseball. This was better than getting my first paycheck at my first job. Hell, this was better than my first engagement! (Now that I think of it, a lot of things have been better than that.) This was the result of consistent work, despite all the stress, fear, and self-doubt that had constantly lurked in the background. I was finally closing and selling my first contract for a profit, and a healthy one at that!

I remember driving to the title company to sign the paperwork and meet with the title agents. The owner of Fireland Title Group, the title company for which I worked, would also be there. His name is Ben. He was the biggest reason I was able to close the deal in the first place. He had taken me under his wing and had spent valuable time slowly shaping me into a productive asset within the local real estate community. He showed me what it meant to problem-solve and to serve others. He taught me that money was the byproduct of good ethical business practices and not the product of self-absorption. I mention him now because you will be hearing more about him throughout this book and will begin to comprehend the power of a great coach.

I vividly remember checking my bank accounts on my mobile app to see if I could buy a cup of coffee before entering the title company's office. The entries I saw for my two accounts are indelibly engraved in my mind:

Savings: $0
Checking: $11

It had been almost a year since I had received my last check from my previous employer. My net worth, for all intents and purposes, was actually negative, given the debts that I had accumulated over the past few years, but at that exact moment I had $11 to my name.

One of my largest motivations is NEVER to feel that pain again. I wanted to run from that feeling of poverty and desperation as fast as I could. I ran up the steps of the title company and took a deep breath before entering the office. I was praying that nothing had gone wrong at the last second, that everything was okay to close. After seeing my life's worth in black and white as $11, I had chosen to skip the celebratory coffee and go straight to closing. The closing for my buyer was scheduled at 11a.m. I was in the office by 10:30.

10:45...

11:00...

11:15 comes and goes;

11:30 and still no buyer.

At this point it took everything I had in me to remain seated and resist breaking down in panic. At 11:30 one of the agents reached out to the buyer and returned explaining that the buyer couldn't get a cashier's check for the closing because his driver's license had expired and he had no other identification on him at the time. So, we requested that he wire the money, but the bank also required a valid driver's license for a wire transaction.

Here's the next best part. This closing was scheduled to happen on a Friday. The buyer had no way of getting his license renewed before Monday morning. This meant the deal was on hold the entire weekend in order to allow the buyer to get everything sorted out and then come in to sign the papers. So here I am, $11 to my name, and I am being forced to wait 72 hours until closing. I had to survive the weekend on $11. Of course, now I'm also worried that the buyer may not be legitimate. That fact and the extent of my financial destitution were colliding around in my head. This is the definition of stress, and it was a serious test of emotional intelligence. I realized I had to manage myself well enough to function and interact with others in order to avoid blowing up the deal. This was a lesson in logical problem-solving and not emotional problem-solving, which I learned much later on.

Fast forward through the weekend to Monday morning. I had signed all of my paperwork the previous Friday and was literally pacing around the house with my phone in my hand, waiting for an update. The buyer was due at the office at 11 a.m. again. It was almost exactly 11 a.m. when the phone rang. It was the title company.

"Deal is done. We're on our way to file it at county now."

It had finally happened. It was real. I had completed a real estate deal. I had earned my first check. I exhaled in what felt like the first time in three days. I was speechless. I had never earned so much credibility with myself in my life. I told myself I was going to do this no matter what. I was going to do this and make this work, or I was going to die.

That is what I told myself, and now I had done it. I had closed my first deal. I received the incoming wire for the profit later in the day. The wire was for just under $7,000, but that $7,000 felt like a million dollars. It was the first real money I had truly earned on my own. I didn't have an employer standing over me, telling me what I had to do for 40 hours a week in order to receive the measly amount of pay they offered. That $7,000 represented truth. It meant freedom. And it accomplished something that is most important for any new entrepreneur to experience. My mind switched from envisioning to acknowledging reality! The deal was real. The money was real. I was real!

It was at that very moment that I realized how important it is to close your first deal, no matter the amount of money involved. Regardless of whether it is $1 or $10,000, you have the ability to look at that check and see for the first time that the possibility of earning a good income in real estate is real and not just some far-flung dream.

The reality of it is not just for those who are posting win after win while you struggle to get a single lead. It's not just for the people who already have flourishing businesses with a lot of money to spend on luxurious items and grand vacations. The reality is there for anyone who's willing to put in a little bit of work and remain consistent through the difficult and frustrating times. It is for you!

If you are reading this and counting the ways that you are different from others who have been successful, you are already wrong. You are no different! The only difference between you and the millionaire you follow on social media is that he or she has put in the time it takes to learn a skill and leverage that skill in order to generate the income he/she needs to live the lifestyle he/she desires. Earning income is simply a skill that you practice. You get better at it over time! When this deal closed for me, the notion of income-generation being a practiced skill smacked me in the face like a freight train! It clicked! *I can do this again!*

---

**GREAT QUESTION: AM I FOCUSING ON MYSELF AND THE PROCESS OF IMPROVING DAY BY DAY, OR AM I COMPARING MYSELF TO OTHERS WHO HAVE BEEN ON THE PATH MUCH LONGER THAN I HAVE?**

---

# HOW LIFE CHANGES FOR THE BETTER AFTER DEAL ONE

I had closed my first wholesale deal. I had more in my bank account after a single closing than I had in the previous months combined. I had a taste for what real estate had to offer. Time to get more!

The cool part about closing a deal for the first time is that it means you have put in the time and work needed to network, organize, sign, and close. And this means that you have already put in the work toward deal number two! I had my second deal signed only a few days after I had closed on my first, and it closed a few weeks after that. I enjoyed the feeling of accomplishment and success once again! I could see myself getting addicted to this feeling. I finally felt like someone who could win rather than simply watch others around me get rich. Looking back, I realize no one around me was really getting rich; they were actually all getting poorer and poorer because they kept investing in "stuff" instead of in assets that would improve their lives.

I will revisit feeling like everyone else is doing better than you later in this book. I will discuss what you should look for in others when you are feeling down on yourself because this is a real feeling that can cripple you and your business. I will teach you a way to avoid this feeling completely and even convert it into a positive energy boost.

I followed my path of constantly marketing, contracting, and selling to a couple of my best buyers for the next 10 to 12 months. I found myself at the closing table multiple times a month; sometimes I even closed multiple deals in a single day. I was solving problems for sellers, and my buyers loved working with me because I was always transparent and honest from the get-go, while providing them a property at a real discount. I was feeling pretty much invincible at that point. Why would I ever want or need to do anything else? I saw no reason ever to change anything in my "business." I was closing all of these deals with virtually no overhead because I had no employees, and my marketing expense was minimal since I had multiple deals coming to me each month using my free advertising strategies that I taught in Book 1 of this series and because my reputation as a problem solver and a real performer was growing in the community.

However, towards the end of this 12-month sprint, I learned that I needed to change, even if it was going to be uncomfortable. My teacher wasn't a mentor; it wasn't a guru getting in my ear about passive income. It was something much more powerful and much more convincing. It was my wife's health. She got sick--and stayed sick--for 10 months straight. When I say sick, I mean bedridden, can't-keep-anything-down, and can-barely-work-from-home sick. She had something called hyperemesis gravidarum. This is a condition wherein you can't eat or drink without getting sick while you're pregnant. We were pregnant with our firstborn!

This was one of the most exciting times of my life as well as some of the most stressful and anxious times of my life all wrapped up into one confusing ball of unknown. I knew one thing for sure, though. I had stopped working completely. I started spending time with my wife and preparing for our son. I finally realized that I hadn't worked on my business in three full months, and our bank accounts were bleeding to death. My buying partners were calling. I was flat out ignoring seller leads and calls. I hadn't been to the title company I had been using to see anyone. I had fallen off the face of the wholesaling business planet.

This was the exact moment that it hit me. I had a job. It was a good paying job, but a job none the less. I was trading my time for money. I wasn't building a flourishing business; I was burning myself out running rampant to visit as many seller leads as possible and network with as many buying partners as possible. I think this was God's way of giving me the greatest gift in the world, my newborn son, packaged with another gift: "Hey! Here's a big ole lesson, too!"

Message received! I needed to change, and I needed to take the steps to do so right away. I could no longer be the person creating the marketing, handling the incoming calls, going on the appointments, signing the contracts, negotiating, meeting the buyers, going to closings, and repeating until the end of time. I needed to create a path to repeat income, asset growth, and team building. I needed to make a transition, and I needed to do it in a way that fit my values and the risk levels that I could tolerate at the time.

With my wife being sick, I was trying to be home as much as possible, so we both agreed that buying our first rental properties at this time didn't make sense for us. We didn't have a team or a management company that we trusted yet. We wanted to make a virtually risk-free transition to repeat and passive income. We managed to accomplish this by holding notes. I began taking promissory notes as payments on my wholesale properties. Instead of asking for five or ten thousand dollars at closing, I took lien positions on the properties and received payments from my buyers over time. I took notes on houses, contracts, and even mobile homes.

At the time I was doing this, mobile home titles were technically just fancy car titles, so I took a secured position and held a clean title while the buyer received a memorandum title until he or she paid off the note. It worked in the same way it works when you buy a car from a dealership using financing. I cover this in full detail later in this book and take you through the step-by-step process so that you can replicate it and scale it to fit your needs.

What this did was secure at least a little bit of income each month to cover our bills so that I didn't have to worry constantly about having to leave my wife to take care of something at work while she was sick at home. I continued with this strategy until Wyatt, my son, was born. We still owned no actual real property at that point in our lives. We never had our name on a title or a deed. We owned debt--which I love! It remains one of my favorite methods for generating passive income, and I still use it.

My goal is to own a billion dollars in notes one day. This is how the banks get so large and so powerful. They are constantly building more income streams via interest payments and principal repayments on the debt they hold. I try to mimic bank activity as much as possible. If I have learned anything throughout this journey, it is that you want to find people successfully doing what you want to do and follow what they have done to create success. In this case, banks own debt. So, I started following their footsteps, and I was able to get more freedom in my life. It really is that simple when you break it down. Try not to overcomplicate things when you are looking to change some aspect of your life. Keep it simple!

After my son was born, we began building our team and creating systems that I will discuss in detail later. We began purchasing property to produce repeat income and to build a strong foundation for a growing portfolio. My mindset shifted from ponds of income to streams of income. I discovered the importance of investing in systems and in people you trust in order to establish a real business, not a struggling job. The lessons I teach in this book are all based on my experiences, which include countless mistakes and adaptations. You won't get very far in business without taking ownership of your failures and mistakes. Only then can you learn from them and discover a new route to follow. I made countless mistakes in building our business, and I still make mistakes today. If you aren't making mistakes, you aren't growing. So, if anyone ever tells you they no longer make mistakes, RUN! This means they are no longer growing, and that's the last person you want to be around.

We now have flourishing and growing investment portfolios with better people and a stronger foundation than we have ever had. We have more time freedom than ever and more options and opportunities as a result. And isn't that the ultimate goal in this wild journey we call life? Let's begin by building your foundation for the future. I will pause my personal story and explain how you can transition from trading your precious time for a measly check to receiving income every single day, even if you choose not to get out of bed.

---

**GREAT QUESTION: AM I TRADING MY TIME FOR INCOME? IF I AM, HOW CAN I TRANSITION OUT OF THIS CYCLE SO THAT I CAN EARN MORE THAN I EVER DREAMED POSSIBLE?**

---

# Money Story

The next sentence may shock you. *People have no idea how money actually works.* Okay, it may not be a shock whatsoever. The problem is that people don't know what they don't know about money. This makes them financially dangerous to the people around them. It is the blind leading the blind.

Asking yourself great questions to improve your life is only one of the themes of this book. The major theme is money flow. The title of this book is *If You Can't Cashflow After This… I've Got Nothing For You* for a reason. You need to build a foundation in financial literacy in order to make money each month and keep it. If you apply the lessons within these pages, you should see immediate improvements in your financial situation.

What if I told you that money wasn't real? Money is simply an agreement. It is an agreed-upon acceptable tender of trade for services or items. Money holds no real value. We hold all the real value within ourselves. If you found that confusing, reread that first line. Money isn't real. If you don't believe me, lay a $1 bill and a $100 bill next to each other. Now, which one is more valuable? Many would say that the $100 bill is more valuable, but in reality, it is identical to the $1 bill. The value of either bill exists only within ourselves because we have the ability to move the dollar bill as we see fit. If the two bills are left lying next to each other, neither will suddenly get up and transform itself into another item or invest itself in something that will grow. Both will simply lie there and collect dust.

You, on the other hand, hold all of the power. You control the money. You control the movement and the flow. Whether you have $1 or $100 in your hand, it doesn't matter. Once you are able to understand this, you will realize that you are the creator of your financial future. You are never controlled by the money, and the money is never the issue. The mind that created a financial issue will never be the same mind that solves the problem. You must adjust and adapt to a new set of principles and thoughts that will enable you to understand that you are the true value and that money is simply a tool for improvement and enjoyment. Spend and move it wisely!

So, if money isn't real, how do we use it, and why does everyone consider it real? The reason money isn't real is because it's backed by nothing. There is no limited quantity of anything special that backs the U.S. dollar. (The principles we address are universal, but we are focusing on the U.S. dollar in this book.) At one point in history the dollar was backed by gold. True money. Real money. The gold standard, as it was called, stabilized the dollar and maintained its value because the dollar was backed by something that is limited in quantity and has its own intrinsic value since it is used in electronics, jewelry, and medical devices, to name just a few alternatives. There is only so much gold available and, under the gold standard, you could exchange your U.S. dollars for gold at a pre-determined fixed price. The U.S. abandoned the gold standard on August 15, 1971. On this day, the dollar was no longer real money, but only a currency. There's a big difference between the two.

Think about the term "currency." Current – moving -- flowing. To prosper you need to keep money (currency) moving in and out of investments and other assets so that your money continues to grow. If you don't, your buying power can be eroded by inflation. Inflation is a hidden tax on your dollar that you don't even realize is hurting you

Let's revisit our example of the $1 bill and the $100 bill. Prior to 1971 when you simply held your money, it maintained its value because it could be exchanged for gold. When the gold standard in the U.S was abandoned, the dollar lost value because the U.S. government had the ability to print an unlimited quantity of dollars with no increase in the demand for dollars.

It is a simple matter of supply and demand. When supply goes up and demand either stays the same or falls, what happens? The price or value of an item decreases. Conversely, when the demand for an item (in this case, the dollar) increases and the supply stays the same (as when the gold standard existed since there is a limited supply of gold), the value of the dollar increases. When the value of a dollar increases, it will take fewer dollars to purchase an item you need or want.

Inflation is defined as an increase in the price of a market basket of goods and services. The U.S. has had inflation, to varying degrees, every year since the gold standard was eliminated in 1971. The inflation rate in 1979 was 13.3%; in 2008, it was 0.1%; and in 2017 it was 2.1%. This means that in 1979, an item that cost $100 at the beginning of the year cost $113.30 at the end of the year. In 2017, it wasn't as bad. An item that cost $100 at the beginning of the year only cost $102.10 at the end of the year.

Some people think that simply putting their money in a savings account is a wise investment. But if you put $100 in a savings account that pays 1% interest a year and inflation is 5% that year, at the end of the year, you will have $101 in your account, but something that cost $100 when you deposited that money will now cost you $105. You actually lost buying power. By saving money and not putting it to use, you are literally losing money. Now that you see it in this light, do you see why keeping money stagnant is dangerous? How can you save if you are constantly losing? You can't! This is why this volume in the series is dedicated to flow and how to build momentum through different niches within real estate. Later in this book I will teach you how our banking system works and how to replicate it so that you have money that you never even had working for you.

**GREAT QUESTION: AM I IN CONTROL OF MY MONEY, OR IS MY MONEY IN CONTROL OF ME?**

# Pond Mentality

What the media and the general public create as a picture of success is something that I refer to as the "Pond Mentality." They picture large lump sums of cash and big sexy checks. This is what a lot of people strive for and dream about, but in reality, those lump sums of money are subject to extremely heavy taxation and losses before ever hitting your bank account. And that is before inflation or spending even enters the picture. This mentality is best explained by returning to the story that I shared earlier in this book. I had been making a comfortable amount of money, but when I no longer had the ability to work as consistently, my income began failing because I was constantly drawing from my single pond of money. I had nothing flowing into this pond. It was continuing to dry up, and I pulled from it week after week without adding anything to it. What happens to a single pond with no streams flowing into it over time? It dries up! Your bank account is your financial pond. If you have no flow of income into it, it dries up.

The idea, that *I will be safe when I have this much saved up*, isn't a realistic or appropriate mindset for creating any sort of cashflow or financial freedom. Financial freedom comes only from turning capital over and over and engaging in actions that keeps your money working for you so that you no longer have to work as long and hard for it. Remember who is in control: you, not the money. When you have a pond mentality, the money will always have control over you. This mentality is short-term thinking and selfish. It is ensuring that you will always have a pond that is fighting you and drying up instead of helping you flourish and grow along with it.

Remember that ponds are still. They have no flow. They simply churn and dry up. Some take longer than others, but at the end of the day, a pond is weak and vulnerable compared to other bodies of water that have many streams flowing in and out of it. I don't see the ocean drying up anytime soon. Think about how many streams and lines flow into an ocean every day. Think of your bank account as a body of water. You want as many strong lines and streams flowing into it as possible so that it is constantly growing stronger and building momentum. Stagnancy is a killer.

---

**GREAT QUESTION: IS MY BANK ACCOUNT MORE LIKE A POND OR AN OCEAN? HOW DO I MAKE IT MORE LIKE AN OCEAN?**

---

# WHY CHECKS JUST DON'T WORK

Weekly or biweekly checks will never be enough. What do I mean when I say this? Think about how a majority of people currently get paid. They trade "X" amount of time for "Y" amount of dollars, right? There is nothing wrong with this if what they are doing during the time they are trading for the money is fulfilling to them. That is a success in my mind. The problem, however, is that even if fulfilled by what they are doing, they are going to struggle financially, which isn't fair. At some point those checks need to turn into something that pays them without their having to trade their time for it. It is the only way to achieve financial freedom, and it is the only way to achieve any sort of viable and consistent cashflow growth in order to stay ahead of inflation, spending, and life events.

Checks are essentially small ponds with only your time and effort flowing into them. The problem with this is that to earn more, you need to work harder, or longer, or both. There is a limit to your ability to do this, however. For one thing, we are human and get tired. The other problem is that each day has only 24 hours. Even if you could work 24 hours a day, which isn't possible, you would still have a built-in ceiling on your income.

Imagine if you had one person working alongside you. Now you each have to work only 12 hours per day to get the same amount done as you yourself working 24 hours. What if you had two people alongside you? You could cut your work hours down even more. The three of you working eight hours could complete the same task and earn the same amount as you did working 24 hours by yourself. What if you had three people? What if you had five people? What if you ended up having 10 people, including yourself, on a team working on the same tasks as you did when working your 24-hour day. Now you would have to work just over two hours per day to complete the same amount of work.

You may have noticed a pattern in the above example. Your time became increasingly freer even while the same amount of work was completed. By the end of the example, you had 22 hours of free time per day. What could you do with an extra 22 hours per day?

Here is the real trick. Read this twice! It is the key to cashflow and financial freedom. What if those 10 people weren't actually people? What if they were the weekly or biweekly checks that you now get? What if you began funneling those checks into small real estate holdings so that your money went to work for you? How long would it take before your money was working so hard for you that you no longer had to work for it? What if you could go to work that you found fulfilling day in and day out and chose that path instead of constantly wondering how to refill your pond? Investing your money is how you leverage the checks you receive today to build freedom for tomorrow. We are in control of our dollars, right? Let's choose a better path for those dollars so that they continue to come back to us, and we no longer have a small pond that dries up week to week. This is the key to escaping the rat race and building massive amounts of time-freedom to explore and live life exactly how you see fit.

What about the high-income earners? The high-income earners are actually at the most risk in my opinion. Have you seen the staggering statistics on the number of lottery winners who end up filing for bankruptcy? They have a huge pond that they let dry up over time. I challenge you to look at high-income earners in traditional fields; do some research on the professional athletes who made millions and millions per year for a number of years and end up failing financially. The issue isn't the amount of money these people are making, but the financial literacy that many lack. They end up with large ponds and no streams to keep them strong. No matter how large the pond, if it is constantly being depleted and never replenished, it will eventually dry up. Time never loses. It is undefeated and will stay undefeated. I will teach you how to build a pond that you can draw from every month while it continues to grow.

**GREAT QUESTION: AM I LIVING CHECK TO CHECK, AND CAN I SEND ONE OF THOSE CHECKS OFF TO WORK FOR ME SO I NO LONGER HAVE TO WORK FOR IT?**

# Building Credibility in Yourself

What I have learned from mentoring thousands of people over the years is that anyone who has not yet started, or is struggling to start, a real estate business is lacking in one specific area. They have all been great people. They all *want* to build financial freedom and massive cashflow in their lives. They all *want* to give more and take better care of their families. They may even have plans about how to accomplish it and understand what needs to be done, but they don't act. This is because they lack credibility in themselves. They don't trust themselves enough to ever start. Having credibility in yourself is simply trusting yourself. The issue goes deeper than this, though. People often times don't know how to build credibility in themselves. I've observed that this is especially the case when someone has had credibility at one point and lost it. That is even more detrimental than never having had it in the first place.

Building credibility in yourself is as simple as learning how to trust yourself. Think about how we build trust with other people in order to replicate that within ourselves. We build trust by showing up and doing exactly what we say we're going to do. That is how others begin to trust us over time, right? It is no different when we're dealing with ourselves.

I commonly find people who think they can fix this overnight. This is impossible. Have you ever truly trusted someone you met that same day? There may be feelings of trust, but you don't consider that person your most trusted contact. And while I'm talking about trusting others, let me point out that when you have trust issues with others, the problem often trickles into self-trust issues as well. Problems with self-credibility and trust are simply impossible to fix in only a day or two. This will take time, but the good news is that you will see progress in just one day. It will increase your credibility in yourself when you get up at or before the time the next morning that you promised yourself you would. So, set a specific time to be up and out of bed. When you complete this task, you will have built a small sliver of credibility within yourself because you did exactly what you said you were going to do.

It may seem simplistic and silly, but that's really all building businesses and freedom in your life requires. Pick out positive and actionable steps each day and repeat them consistently day in and day out until you are moving in the direction you want to be moving. When you begin to develop self-credibility, you will experience significant changes in your life. You will find confidence. You will find trust. You will find energy and action. It all begins with credibility in yourself.

Credibility in yourself translates to everything else in your life, not just real estate and business. It will manifest itself in your finances, your relationships, and your day-to-day fulfillment. When you build credibility and confidence in yourself, a certain level of momentum will welcome itself into your life, and you will feel unstoppable. You will feel unstoppable because you will be unstoppable! So, set a time for tomorrow morning that is a half an hour earlier than you normally rise. See how you feel immediately after getting up earlier. I bet you'll feel better than you did the day before.

What are some other ways that we can build credibility in ourselves? What if we are confident in what we do on a daily basis, but we still haven't seen the changes that we want? What if we are working our job but find ourselves on the couch after work, or going through the motions like everyone else on the weekends? How can we jettison this cycle and replace it with something new?

We first need to understand why we do what we do day in and day out. Why is it that we come home and sit on the couch? Why do we do things that we don't really want to do? Is it because we're addicted, or because we feel there is nothing else? The reason may actually surprise you. We end up in these lazy and unproductive cycles because of our ancient subconscious brain. We create habit loops over time, and our brain locks these loops in for survival. We are wired to survive, not to thrive. That being said, our brains know exactly what we did the day before, and our brains know that we survived. Since we survived the prior day, our brains automatically throw us into a loop of similar and same actions because they want to survive another day. All the while you may be sitting there thinking, *Do I want to survive another day like this?*

I know that's what I was asking myself when I was first trying to get going, and I had no idea what was going on inside my head. This is why people stay in poor conditions and bad situations. Their brain doesn't necessarily realize it's bad. It only recognizes that it survived and for it to survive again tomorrow, it should do the same thing. This phenomenon makes change extremely scary. If you sit for too long before acting, your brain fills the unknown space with fear, which reverts you to the same miserable loop as the day before. On the flip side, if you act on a new thought before the brain can recognize it, the brain will actually fill this new unknown space with thoughts of excitement and exploration. The brain cannot be fearful and explore at the same time.

Now that you know why it can be difficult to change and build credibility in yourself, when you find yourself stuck in an unproductive cycle, you can recognize it and abort it before it takes hold. Awareness is key in these situations, and it takes practice. Even if you succeed at stopping the cycle only one time in the first week, you will know that you did manage to stop it once, and this will instill you with confidence that you will be able to change, given time. We have malleable minds, not fixed minds. By focusing on the progression journey, you will be able to build credibility in yourself slowly over time, and before you know it, you will have new habits that fulfill you, which, in turn, sets you up for massive success.

---

**GREAT QUESTION: HOW CAN I BUILD CREDIBILITY IN MYSELF SO THAT I CAN BEGIN GAINING FINANCIAL FREEDOM AS SOON AS HUMANLY POSSIBLE?**

---

# How to Shift Perspective

To create a life of repeat and constant cashflow, you must shift your mind and perspective from today to tomorrow and beyond. Creating ponds and lump sums of cash is planning for today. Creating cashflow and long-term repeat income is planning for tomorrow, next year, and even future generations. Remember when I asked how much different your life would be if your last name was Rockefeller in my first book (*If You Can't Wholesale After This, I've Got Nothing For You…*)? Rockefeller is someone who planned for the future, and not just today. There was nothing special about him. He simply practiced different techniques. You can do the same and create long-term wealth for your family and friends.

When you're thinking about your next paycheck, you are thinking short term. Here are some examples of this type of thinking: *I need to pay this bill by Tuesday. I need to save this much to get this item. I have a trip coming up so I want to get this. Rent is due tomorrow. What can I do to fix this one thing (or item) today or tomorrow?* If you find yourself asking questions or making statements like these, I can all but guess what your financial status and your businesses look like.

Short-term thinkers also commonly use words and phrases like "expensive," "too much," "can't," "impossible," "I wish," "must be nice," "lucky," "but," "I can't wait until the weekend," "hate Monday," and "never." These are all small-minded and short-term thinking comments that scream scarcity in life instead of abundance and long-term vision.

I have found that the most successful people are always journey and progress oriented; they don't waste time looking for a specific point on which to

## IF YOU CAN'T CASHFLOW AFTER THIS

hang their "success hat." They are all working on a long-term purpose and passion rather than searching for an "out" that will allow them to quit and retire. To become your fullest self you must adopt a mindset that embraces the suffering and excitement of the journey as one. A short-term thinker begins his or her journey over every day, never making it past 24 hours. In contrast, a long-term thinker with a mindset focused on progression finds him or herself evolving daily and growing beyond other's expectations of them.

It's easy to take a single action one day and feel progress and fulfillment when it is laser-focused on a long-term path, while the exact opposite is true for short-term thinking and lack of planning or pursuing. You may feel that working 24 hours a day isn't enough to accomplish what you need to do and that it will start all over again the next day. Have you ever felt this before? If so, it is due to a lack of long-term perspective on your life.

Let me give you a more tangible example, using specific numbers and a sequence of financial investments. If I asked you for $5,000 a month, and I promised to return only $2,500 of it per month the first year, would you take that deal? I'm sure most would say no. What if, in the second year, I promise to return $3,500 of your $5,000 per month? Would you take the investment now? No, probably not.

This is where most people would stop listening, if they even made it to my year-two proposal. They would never consider discussing this loan arrangement again. Unfortunately for them, the entire $5,000 that they invested every month would be returned to them each month in year three, and every year following that. Each month that they invested $5,000 a month, they would receive exponentially more until they reached the point wherein they would get $50,000 back PER MONTH for every $5,000 monthly investment. Only the long-term thinker would ever consider this. Someone with a short-term perspective would have dismissed it without thinking about what it might produce for him or her in the long run. The long-term thinker makes an exponential-growth wealth investment that will last him and his family the rest of his life and beyond. This is a simple lesson in something called compound interest. Most miss out on investments like these because they aren't aggressive enough due to their short-sighted perspective. They see only the loss at the beginning and reject the idea outright, missing huge opportunities in the near future.

If this sounds like you, it is time to make an uncomfortable switch from instant to delayed gratification. Delayed gratification is one of the most powerful determining factors in your financial success. The longer you delay gratification and allow growth to occur, the better off you will be in the long run, especially when investing.

Before you can flip your gratification switch, you need to be aware of who you are today. Is the paycheck you receive on Friday gone before the weekend is over? Are you a resolute saver, but too afraid to invest your money? When you are considering an expenditure, do you look for something that will provide you with a return, or do you often spend your money on something that will give you only short-term satisfaction, like a pair of shoes, which will wear out?

If you are someone who looks for items that return money to you, like real estate or other tangible investments, you are practicing delayed gratification. Rather than buying the shoes today for $200, you are putting the $200 into an investment that will, in time, give you the $200 you need to buy the shoes and then continue to pay you for as long as you own it. This is why real estate is so powerful. If you needed $30,000 to buy a car, but instead spent the $30,000 on a piece of real estate that produced $500 a month, that property would make your monthly car payment for you, and when the car was paid off, the real estate would still be working for you and paying you. That's how you scale to freedom! That's delayed gratification.

Many times, simply becoming aware of your current state of mind regarding gratification is enough to enable you to switch to a better long-term plan. Again, like building credibility in yourself, this is a practice. There will be times where you revert back to short-term thinking and instant gratification, but overall you will be aware of what the better financial choices are. It will be uncomfortable at first, but given time, you will begin thinking long term without even realizing it, and you will have difficulty spending on less valuable items that don't build your wealth. This is a good thing! Welcome it into your life. You are building better and more positive habit loops.

A key to shifting perspective to the long-term permanently is to know your ultimate purpose. This takes time to discover. It takes mistakes and pain. It takes trying different things and really figuring out who you are as a person and what impact you want to make on the world. Once you discover it, you need to focus on this defined objective and take purposeful actions towards that goal every single day. Focusing and adapting daily will instill you with feelings of growth and fulfillment and ultimately allow you to shift your perspective and create wealth by concentrating on the journey and making better decisions.

If, while reading that last paragraph, you thought to yourself that you want it to proceed faster than that… hint, hint…

I want to share with you a mental game that I practice to ensure that I am always thinking and focusing on the long-term growth of myself, family, and companies to safeguard our future success. Short-term gains are always sexy. Short-term gains and rewards are always fulfilling for a day or two, but they always fizzle out just as quickly as they came. That's how you can recognize a short-term choice over a long-term opportunity.

When I want to make a decision to move forward, I always practice thinking about the people around me. I think about my son. Will my son be affected by this decision in 20 years? Will my wife benefit from this decision in the next decade? Will the next generation in my family feel the impact of this decision? If the answer is no, which will sometimes be the case because not every decision is going to be life changing, I consider why. If it's a smaller decision, or a decision that involves an experience, such as a trip to The Magic Kingdom, I remind myself that we need to be living life to the fullest, and it's okay to take action. If the decision is a larger decision that involves the direction or future of the people around me and the answer is no, I immediately know that my decision is for short-term gain, and I avoid it. Now, if the answer to my question about the effect on the people around me is yes, I evaluate how it will benefit them in 10, 20, 30 or even 100 years. If I have a choice to make and I see that an action I can take will enable my family's wealth and security to grow over time, I take that road every time, even if it will cause short-term discomfort,

A great way to recognize whether your focus is long-term is to ask yourself how you will feel when taking the first steps on a new path. If the first few steps will be uncomfortable and painful, that is a great sign that you should be taking this new action. Let me explain. There are different tiers and levels to cause and effect. Working out at the gym is a simple example. If you decide to start exercising, you will notice that the first couple of days are extremely uncomfortable and difficult. This is the first result of your initial decision. Tier one. If you continue exercising daily, the discomfort disappears and the results start to show as a leaner, healthier, sexier body. This is tier two. The decision you made was a long-term decision. You embraced the suffering at the outset for the long-term gain of better health. This is no different from any other decision in your life.

When you begin zeroing in on the fact that initial pain will result in long-term comfort, you will have an epiphany and experience the mind shift that you are seeking. Focusing on finding joy in short-term discomfort in return for long-term improvements is life changing. This allows you to keep your purpose and ultimate world impact in mind while freeing you up to take the day-to-day actions needed to make your dreams become reality. When you shift your perspective to long term, you will have the ability to brush off "bad" days because you will feel fulfillment and progress, even during the most difficult times. This shift will introduce better habits and momentum into your life, which will, in turn, become the new norm and bring big-time results.

---

**GREAT QUESTION: AM I FOCUSED ON MY DAY-TO-DAY PROGRESSION AND GROWTH WHILE REMAINING FOCUSED ON MY JOURNEY, OR AM I WORRIED ABOUT ONLY TODAY?**

---

# CREATING MONEY OUT OF THIN AIR

The next big question is this: if we are going to be focused on the long term and create long-term wealth and time-freedom, how do we stop trading time for money? That's a great question! I am glad you thought of it.

If we are focusing on the flow of cash in our lives to create time-freedom, we need to learn how to create money out of thin air. To do this, we need to understand what creating money out of thin air means. The key to money and capital creation is understanding that people pay you money for a solution to their problems. All transactions are simple solutions to different-sized problems. When you pay $450 for a plane ticket to another state, you are provided a solution to traveling a long distance in a short amount of time. The airline is solving a time-constraint problem. When you buy a $1 hamburger from a fast food restaurant, you are provided a solution to your need to eat quickly and on the go. When you pay $30,000 for a car at the dealership, the dealership has provided you a solution to a transportation problem. These are all problems of varying sizes for which you are being provided solutions in exchange for money.

This is the basis of your business and how you create long-term wealth through real estate. Understanding this foundation will enable your mind to see the invisible in transactions and create wealth from them. What solutions can you provide to sellers, buyers, renters, investors, and others to create capital and long-term wealth that will last for generations? How skilled can you become at the process of problem solving, and how efficient can your team become at acting on these principles?

Let me give you an example that you may have missed. Elon Musk founded a company called Tesla. Many people know this. What many people don't realize, though, is that Elon's ultimate goal is to create a cleaner, more efficient earth. He is doing this by creating companies that produce luxury items, such as cars, for which people pay large amounts of money. He is creating money out of thin air for his cause by selling cars.

Cars are typically a large source of pollution. How many people saw the potential for cars to help solve air pollution problems? Not many is the answer! They would need to be able to see and understand the possibility of creating money out of thin air for a deeper cause. Most people would have established a company with a cleaner air slogan and would have attempted to sell an expensive item to combat the issue directly. Elon saw potential when he observed consumers buying cars at astounding rates, and he plugged his cause into the solution. Incredible. This is the type of thinking that will take your life to the next level.

The next step in selling and creating unlimited income through problem solving involves shifting from focusing on the direct product as a sale and, instead, concentrating on the end result, much like fostering cleaner air with cleaner vehicles.

Below is a statement that gave me a whole new perspective on things when I heard it. It is incredibly simple, but if you really study it, you will begin to understand how to look at problem solving and capital creation.

**"No one goes into the hardware store wanting a quarter-inch drill bit; they go into the hardware store to buy a quarter-inch drill bit because they want a quarter-inch hole."** – Jay Samit

When I heard this I nearly fell out of my chair because it pulled everything together for me. People don't want to learn about finances. They want relieved of their credit card debt. People don't want to spend on a college education; they want more opportunity in life. People want the freedom that options provide.

Let's apply Jay Samit's statement to Tesla. Elon was able to achieve his ultimate goal, creating a cleaner earth, by focusing on what people actually want, a nice car that is reliable, stylish, and eco-friendly. Tesla focused on what people wanted in order to achieve what Musk truly wanted. This is a win-win situation. People didn't want a new way of filtering pollution; they wanted a new stylish vehicle to enjoy. Elon and Tesla didn't sell the drill bit; they sold the quarter-inch hole!

Think about that for a bit. In what other areas of your life are you trying to sell the drill bit and not the quarter-inch hole? Maybe, just maybe, a shift in perspective will help turn a failing financial situation around.

So how can you apply this to real estate? How can you speak to a seller and consider a solution to his or her problem unless you understand that they don't want or need money necessarily? They want what they perceive the money will get them. Freedom of options. Now ask yourself how you can provide a seller with that without ever taking a dime out of your own pocket. I did it. I bought a house for $2,500 when it was worth $30,000 and then sold it for over $40,000! I provide a case study on this house later in this book for your edification. The best part about that deal is that it has continued to pay me month after month, like clockwork, without any risk or responsibility.

---

**GREAT QUESTION: AM I SELLING THE QUARTER-INCH DRILL BIT, OR AM I SELLING THE SOLUTION TO A QUARTER-INCH HOLE?**

---

# How to Eliminate Trading Time for Income to Set Yourself Free

Now that you understand the mindset that underlies creating transactions and creating value in other people's lives by providing solutions to different problems, let's cover the actionable steps needed to stop trading your time for income. Trading time for income comes in all sorts of different shapes and sizes. Many believe that if they own the company, they aren't trading their time for income. Some believe that when they own the real estate, managing the property themselves isn't trading their time for income. These are both examples of owning jobs. Just like me in the story I shared at the beginning of this book, you aren't building a business if the business is built around you. If the day-to-day operations don't continue to run smoothly whether you are working or not, then you have more outsourcing and systems to create. It is irresponsible to have a business that is dependent on your working in it every day. Notice I said *in* it and not *on* it.

The only way to achieve true financial and time freedom is to build a business in which you own the systems within it. Each property you own is its own little business, with income, expenses, management, maintenance, accounting, and financials. When you build a business around yourself, you cripple the growth potential and you create a built-in income ceiling. This is because you have only so much time to trade throughout the day, as I discussed previously.

The best way to visualize this it to ask yourself, *If I had 50 more of these, what would my life look like?* every time a problem arises in your business. If the answer is anything but "good," you know that you need more balance and more systems in place. If you own a rental property and the tenant is failing to pay and you must evict them, what does that look like for you over the next 30 to 45 days? Are you the one posting the notice on the door? Are you the one communicating with the tenant? Are you going to the courthouse with the attorney? Are you at each eviction on the move-out day? If you answered yes to these, imagine having 50 more at the same time. Does that sound like financial or time freedom? I don't think so!

Our goal is to create flourishing investments that maintain and grow on their own. When we are able to achieve repeat income in a manner that others who are trustworthy can manage, we are free to pursue life as we see fit. We then have the time and financial resources to make the impact on the world that we envisioned throughout this journey. So how do we do this, you ask? We start, and we start right now! We begin trusting others. We begin learning how to train and influence others in the way that we think and feel so that we can work together in a common direction toward a mutual goal while providing opportunities for others.

Let me give you a specific example using one of my own properties wherein my team handled everything from the technical analysis of the purchase to managing the tenant and collecting rent. One of the niches of my business focuses on single family properties with no plumbing on the second floor. My mentor Ben taught me long ago that plumbing on the second floor causes more problems than it solves. As a result, my team loves ranch-style homes with small yards that keep maintenance and utility costs to a minimum.

My acquisitions manager got a lead from an online ad that had been posted. He reviewed the type of lead and determined why the seller wanted to sell. He qualified the property and the lead based on the fact that there was a problem we had the ability to solve. He then contacted another team member and requested that he walk the property and meet the seller. This team member went to the property, confirmed the verbally-stated condition of the house, and made an offer that fit our criteria. The seller accepted the offer, and the two signed a purchase agreement in the company name. The signed paperwork was then sent to our title company (Fireland Title

Group in Hudson, Ohio) to initiate escrow and complete the paperwork for closing. Once the paperwork was completed, the title company contacted all parties for final signatures, and the money was wired to the title company to be dispersed to the seller. After closing, my managing team member reached out to the tenant and set up a meeting to explain expectations.

Throughout this entire process I was only contacted two times. Once for confirmation that I wanted the property and once for closing. Now what would my life look like if I had 50 more of these? My life would look great! This is a prime example of how easy life can be if you have trustworthy people helping you build a business. If I had to handle everything myself, I wouldn't be able to execute more than a deal or two every few months. It would be too hectic, especially when--not if--problems arose. This property is now managed and coordinated by the internal team that we have built. Whether you build your own management team or outsource to a third party is up to you, as long as your team members are trusted and organized for productivity and serve the tenants and you equally.

Here is the truly beautiful part about the process above. Not only was I only contacted two times, but this property will pay me and my family forever. Literally forever. The process described has set my family up for success for generations. This is the art of building and owning systems that continue to pay you even though the process only has to be completed once.

Now the question becomes how many properties or deals can your process handle at once? If your process is struggling and team members are frustrated, you won't be able to do many deals. If your process is set up to run smoothly with specific tasks for each member so that they aren't spread too thin, there is a great chance that you can do multiple deals per month. Now think about what this will look like over time, assuming you can get paid forever for processing a property just one time. If you complete just one property deal per month in the beginning and each property pays you $500 a month, you will have created 12 new lines of income after the first year. This means you will be earning you $6,000 in repeat income before any expenses you may have.

Now what if you do three property deals per month? 6? 12? 15? (Remember this is just a process of providing a solution to someone, so you will get better and better at it.) If you complete three transactions per month, at the end of 12 months you will have created $18,000 in repeat income per month. Of course, there are always unexpected problems that can crop up in your business that you will have to solve, but I want you to envision what's possible when you shift your mind from trading your time for income to creating systems that will create money out of thin air for you over and over again. The scale is endless. You can take it as far as you wish!

At the end of the day the answer to scaling without having to scale massive amounts of time and operations is in your business planning. Are you attempting to scale something that can be repeated many times per day without automation? If so, you are always going to struggle to hit any sort of momentum or stride because time is the ultimate equalizer. It cannot be overcome unless automation can be increased. The only way to automate processes is through systems and technology. Let me ask you a question. If you mail a check for rent on your apartment, what happens on the other end? Do you see that as automated on the business side? I don't. It will require manpower and time, the ultimate equalizer to scale, to retrieve the check from the mail, open the check, deposit the check, record it as received, and then file it. These are all pieces that must be automated to scale at a massive level. In our business we require that payments be made electronically through our online management system. This ensures the customer that his or rent payment is safely received, automatically recorded, filed, and tracked, and the tenant also gets a receipt. The technology we use even records the income into our financial statements to update our books, which are then sent to our accountants for tax purposes. You know how long this takes? SECONDS! No one has to lift a finger, and no one has to clock in or out. What if you had 50 more of these? Life would look great! This is what freedom of time and scale looks like. This is all possible through your business planning.

―――――

**GREAT QUESTION: AM I BUILDING A BUSINESS AROUND MYSELF, OR AM I BUILDING A BUSINESS OUTSIDE OF MYSELF?**

―――――

# An Intro to Understanding How to Earn Money Passively

Earning money passively is a skill that is practiced and mastered over time. Let me repeat that. Earning money passively is a skill that is practiced and mastered over time. It takes practice to earn income passively through system building and asset acquisition. To truly understand how to earn repeated income you must comprehend the differences between two basic financial principles. Assets and liabilities are accounting terms that you must understand if you want not only to earn money passively, but to get financially free. These two are the main factors in your flow of cash month to month. Assets are designed to provide you some sort of financial benefit, whether it be now or in the future, and liabilities create a financial obligation. Liabilities are money you owe. Assets pay you, and liabilities take from you. Income and expenses.

You can probably guess which of these you should have more of if you want to build a life with a lot of time-freedom and options. The problem is that we are raised with and surrounded by constant attacks on our ego and self-worth through marketing that encourages us to increase our liabilities to keep our social status high. The general approach of these constant bombardments is "buy this or feel like less." So, we end up spending money that we usually don't even have to purchase items that give our brains a short-term hit of dopamine, which creates excitement. The problem is that this little burst of happiness is extremely short-lived. As quickly as the excitement of owning something new comes, it leaves us--wanting more and feeling a little emptier than previously. This creates a cycle of spending as we try to keep up with our own bad habits by working longer and working harder. Does this sound familiar?

When we reach this advanced stage of social anxiety, we are fully emerged in working long and hard hours in trade for items that don't fulfill us. Blame is the next step in this cycle. We don't blame ourselves--of course not--we blame others! We blame our boss; we blame the company we work for; we blame the market. We justify by saying the company we work for doesn't pay us enough. We create a story in our minds that allows us to feel victimized by the tough markets, and we turn to politics and others for comfort. This is why we see so much negative press on money and business. The reality is that our problems are internal. They are our own. We must take ownership of the financial decisions that we have made. Once this happens, we have the ability to open up and receive new information and new lines of income to solve our problems. Then and only then will any financial improvements be made.

With that being said, say aloud, **"My financial situation is 100% my fault, and my fault alone."**

Now that our minds are open, we can fully understand how to apply the basics of earning income passively. We now understand that the choices we make will be manifested in the results that we receive, and that our financial stability is dependent only on our choices. Our situation in life will be determined by the sum of the actions that we take. Understanding this is key to earning repeat income in the future because it shifts your mind's perspective from "time traded for X amount of dollars" to "value provided equals X amount of dollars." This shift in perspective will open the door to receiving income for completing a process only once instead of having to show up each and every hour and getting paid only for the hours worked.

A great question you can ask yourself is, "Will this item return the same amount of money to me after purchase, or will I have to re-earn this money after purchasing it?" If the answer is ever anything other than a positive return on your money, you should consider another purchase. Assets continue to pay you over time. Liabilities are fine as long as the asset you purchase with the debt will pay off the debt and then some. I will touch on this in more detail soon.

In summary, your focus should be on long-term growth through assets that pay you many, many times over the course of your life. In the upcoming sections, I will discuss a number of methods to accomplish this in the real estate industry. Real estate is one of the greatest options for passive income because it provides so many unique ways for you to be paid over time. Real estate holdings generate monthly rent payments and provide you with growth potential through price appreciation. There's nothing quite like spending on an item one time and getting paid multiple times a month in multiple fashions. This is an incredible way to speed up your currency flow and increase your net worth and cashflow at the same time.

Our focus throughout this book will continue to be cash flow, but net worth is the value of all your assets minus your liabilities. So, if you own a million dollars in real estate, and you only owe $300,000 on those assets, your net worth from real estate would be $700,000. There are other assets and liabilities that factor into your net worth, but our focus here is on real estate, and I want to keep it simple.

To begin earning passive income, you also need to understand what cashflow looks like. If your income currently equals your expenses, your cashflow is zero. This is no way to live. This is the rat race at its finest. You want your income to be well above your expenses. This is how you can escape the rat race and create options for yourself. To do this you first need to determine what your current income and expenses are. It's okay if your cashflow is breakeven right now, or even below zero and in the red. This is why you are reading this book! We can improve this together. Let me show you a quick example:

Income: $5,000 per month

Expenses $3,000 per month

Monthly positive cashflow is $2,000

See how simple this can be? Don't overcomplicate this process. Good business is simple business. Simple business allows us to scale, earn repeat income, and build flourishing real estate portfolios from many different angles!

The final piece to welcoming passive income into your life is to understand that it is the key to escaping the rat race, and, as such, it needs to be your main focus at all times. Every time you earn just a few more repeat dollars per month, you get closer to the point at which your income will exceed your expenses without your having to work day in and day out. This thought should help you focus on the progression of the journey instead of lump sum payments and trading your time for money. This is an exciting shift to undertake!

---

**GREAT QUESTION: AM I CREATING ASSETS THAT PAY ME OVER TIME, OR AM I CREATING A LIFE THAT REQUIRES ME TO WORK FOR MY INCOME DAY TO DAY?**

---

# Using Promissory Notes to Build Wealth

What is a promissory note? A promissory note is a document that is signed by two parties with an agreement stating that Party 1 agrees to pay Party 2 a set amount of money over a specific amount of time. This is a legally binding agreement that enables you to receive multiple payments over a period of time instead of receiving a single lump sum when you sell a piece of property or an interest in a property.

The note stipulates all the terms, such as the principal (the amount being borrowed, the interest rate, and the amount and frequency (monthly, quarterly, annually) of each payment. This gives a very clear and concise picture to both the seller and buyer. The seller understands how much to expect in payment each period and when to expect it, while the buyer understands what obligations he or she has, including when the debt must be paid in full. When you own a promissory note, you own debt. You are the lender, and the borrower is said to have sold you the promissory note (debt). When banks lend you money to buy a property, car, or on a personal loan, they are buying your debt.

When a bank lends you money to purchase a property, they create a mortgage. The mortgage, stipulating the terms of the transaction, is signed by both you and the bank and is recorded above the deed of the property. This is commonly referred to as a security position. If you fail to pay the bank the agreed upon amount at the specified times, the bank can take ownership of the property. An individual property seller can do the same thing. If you own property and finance your buyer's purchase of it and the

# IF YOU CAN'T CASHFLOW AFTER THIS

buyer fails to pay you according to the terms of the note, you can retake ownership of the property and control it again. This is called secured debt. You are owed a monthly payment (assuming the parties have agreed upon monthly payments) and are not responsible for the property anymore. Your only job is to cash a check each month. Sounds like a good deal, right? As I mentioned earlier, this is how I initially built my freedom. There are pros and cons to this type of investment, however.

Promissory notes are really very simple agreements that help you create wealth and consistent cashflow over time because they enable you to receive years and years of payments by completing just a single transaction. Notes are also negotiable, which make them very flexible assets that you can control for pennies on the dollar, and sometimes there are no out-of-pocket costs involved.

When you own secured debt, you can typically sell that debt just like you can a piece of real estate. You are owed "X" amount of dollars over a specific amount of time, and you can sell that agreement and that debt to another entity for a lump sum, barring any securities regulations forbidding the resale. This provides you with the flexibility to move in and out of investments, which can be important.

"Why would I ever want to sell a promissory note for a lump sum that is less than what I am owed?" There are a number of reasons that selling debt may make sense, but a common one is so that you can immediately reinvest the money received into another investment that will grow and pay you more monthly than the current note pays you. Here's an example: You own a secured note with a principal amount of $20,000 that pays you $200 per month. An opportunity arises wherein if you invest $15,000 in a different promissory note, you will receive $500 per month, and the total principal on that note is $50,000. You would willingly give up $5,000 for a $300-per-month bump in income and a $30,000 increase in debt owned. This means you just traded $5,000 for a return of $30,000. Not bad! This is what is possible with promissory notes.

If you don't know how banks work, pay close attention and read this section multiple times if need be. No one is better at creating wealth than banks. No one. When I wanted to create freedom for myself, I asked myself how I could act more like a bank every day. There are some key points to understand about our banking systems that will enable to make better financial choices.

The United States, along with most of the rest of the world, uses a fractional reserve banking. This means that when the bank receives a deposit of money, it only needs to hold a percentage of that money as cash; the rest can be used to make loans. At the time of writing this the banks, the reserve requirement on checking accounts is 10%. So, if you deposit $100 into your checking account, the bank must keep $10 of it as cash and can lend out the other $90. Loans create new money in our economy and are, thus, expansionary. Speaking in larger terms, the bank can lend $90,000 for every $100,000 deposit it has. That $90,000 may be lent out as car loans, business loans, mortgages, or any combination thereof. This creates a lot of options for the banks and multiple exit plans and lines of income.

I want you to think about doing this one time. I will teach you how to negotiate a secured loan on property you don't even own, and I will teach you how to do it without risking any capital beyond that needed to purchase the property. Think about how your life would be different if you had the ability to create money out of thin air like this. Now think about the scale at which banks are doing this. The banks are practicing this, thousands and thousands of times per day. Now, that is wealth generation!

I want to follow that road as closely as I can to replicate their results and create generational wealth just as the banks do. When I am looking to create wealth and make moves with my investments, I seek out others already successful in the field and replicate their actions to get similar results. Who better to follow in note and wealth creation than the banks? What if I told you that we could do it even cheaper than the banks can? They need to hold 10% in reserves; we need zero! Now, I am not saying that there are no regulations or rules to follow because there are, and we will cover those, but I want your mind shifting to creating massive wealth with minimal risk.

Promissory notes are incredible assets that will always be viable options for entering or exiting a property transaction for maximum profits with minimal risk. Notes create time-free cashflow and help grow wealth over time while building a consistent income. Pairing notes with other types of assets and investments gives you the ability to build a diverse real estate portfolio protected from economic movements and downtimes. At the end of the day you are either going to get monthly payments or own the property. It is win-win.

Remember, as a rule of thumb, you want to own secured debt—debt that is backed by real property. This is what protects you. Furthermore, you should heavily consider only investing in debt on property when you are in a $1^{st}$ lien position. This means if the borrower defaults on the loan or sells the property, you get paid first. There can be an unlimited amount of lien positions. If you are second, third, fourth or deeper, you risk not getting paid if someone defaults and the property isn't worth enough to cover the lien positions that are ahead of yours in their entirety. We want minimal risk, so consider only working with $1^{st}$ lien-position properties. Let's look at a couple of examples:

Example 1: The property is worth $100,000. You are in $1^{st}$ lien position with a note of $80,000. The owner of the property must sell, and he sells the property for $90,000. You receive your $80,000 first, and then the seller receives the remaining amount.

Example 2: The property is worth $100,000. You are $2^{nd}$ lien position with a $10,000 promissory note while another lender is in $1^{st}$ position with a $90,000 note. The owner must sell. The house fails to sell for $100,000, and sells instead for $95,000. You are at risk of not being repaid the full $10,000 because $100,000 is owed but only $95,000 is available. The $1^{st}$ position lender will receive his $90,000 before you will receive anything.

We always want to focus on our risk and reward. If we own debt on a property that is worth more than what is owed and we are in first position, we are extremely safe. We can count on the fact that we will either receive regular monthly income, or, if need be, can foreclose on the property and resell it for a profit. Subordinate positions, as illustrated in the examples above, increase our risk. Don't be afraid to pass on deals that put you in deeper lien positions. Just because you have the ability to do the deal doesn't mean that you should.

---

**GREAT QUESTION: AM I ACTING IN LINE AND FOLLOWING THE FOOTSTEPS OF OTHER WEALTHY ENTITIES, OR AM I TRYING TO REINVENT THE WHEEL AND RISKING MORE THAN NECESSARY?**

---

# The Pros of Owning Promissory Notes

As mentioned previously, there are pros and cons to every investment and every investment style. It is important to note that there are far more positives to owning debt for passive income. Let's touch on a handful here.

1. **No Responsibility**

    The largest and most noticeable reason for investing in secured promissory notes is that you have absolutely no responsibility whatsoever for the property or the management of it, but you still get paid every month. Whether you are dealing with an investor-controlled or an owner-occupant property doesn't affect when or how you get paid. If the property is vacant, you are due your payment. If the property is losing money monthly for the investor, you are due payment. If the owner-occupant decides to sell, you get paid first.

    You have no responsibility for property taxes. You never need to see the property or worry about it beyond confirming that the borrower is carrying the requisite amount of insurance on it. You want to be certain the borrower has the proper amount of insurance so that you are protected in case of loss. The number one goal of investing in notes is to secure your money. With proper coverage and the right borrower, you have low risk exposure, while profiting each month. You will have zero hours per month involved in creating cashflow. This frees you up to create more and more income without having to scale your time involvement. This is why I love owning debt so much!

2. **Consistent for years**

   The terms of a promissory note can be negotiated at the outset, but remember that we are focusing on long-term gains and growth. The longer your money is in play, the more you earn over time with interest. Interest is the key to scaling your money and growth over time. Even more important than the interest rate in this scenario is the total amount of interest you will be earning. There is a reason banks lend for 30 years! They more than double their money by doing this.

   Think about it this way. Would you rather earn 10% on your money for 12 months or 144 months? The difference between profit on strictly interest in that scenario on a $100,000 principal is a mind boggling $66,592.21. That's right, if you lend over a 12-year term instead of 1 year you will earn $66,592.21 more! When your lending term is only 1 year, you earn $5,499.06 in interest. Not a bad return for 12 months! If you aren't practicing the long-term thinking skills that we've been discussing, you may jump at that! The problem is that if you sit back and decide to lend for the long term, you will earn $72,091.27 in interest payments. Which would you like to earn? Do you see why the banks lend for such long periods of time? People think it is because it lowers the monthly payments for them and makes the loan more affordable. Wrong! It is because the bank earns more. Banks are for-profit entities, not charities.

   Investing in promissory notes for long-term growth is an incredibly consistent and reliable way to build new wealth. When you are creating long-term wealth, you want to build it on a strong foundation. One of the best ways to do so is by earning income every month with no worries of loss of income without security.

3. **Flexible and Liquid**

   Owning a promissory note is much like owning a real tangible object. You are due the money that is specified in the terms of that note. This makes promissory notes great tools for collateral and liquidity. You can move in and out of promissory notes with relatively less work than buying and selling property. If you own a $50,000 note, you have the ability to sell that note to another investor or entity, assuming it does not violate any applicable security laws. This gives you the option to cash out whenever you deem it necessary. Having that kind of control and flexibility in your investments is key to success. Promissory notes are simply more tools that allow you to control income and the rate at which it flows to you.

4. **Tax Benefits**

Real estate is well known for its tax benefits. To understand all of the tax benefits that real estate can bring you, I recommend you consult an experienced CPA, but I want to explain a basic principle to you. Everyone knows that there are different tax brackets and tax rates. A traditional W2 earner at a job is taxed heavier than anyone. Being smart and owning debt allows you to avoid giant lump-sum tax threats. When you sell a property that you have rehabbed and make $100,000 on it, you are at risk of paying heavy capital gain taxes on the full profit. When you receive payments on the promissory notes you own, you pay taxes only on the interest income that you have received. Let's suppose you receive $12,000 a year in interest payments. Would you rather pay tax on $100,000 upfront or on $12,000 each year? Once again, promissory notes create more options for you.

5. **Fight Inflation**

Inflation is defined as a general increase in price levels and a fall in the purchasing value of money. As price levels increase, your buying power decreases. This is a simple lesson in supply and demand. When you have money sitting in the bank, it is losing value every single day. On the other hand, if you invest your money in notes, your money is earning whatever interest rate is specified on the note. If you have $100,000 in a 12-year note, as stated before, you earn $72,091.27 and your $100,000 is now somewhere near $172,091.21 in terms of true value. If you have your money "saved" in a bank, you would think that after 12 years, you would have $100,000 in true value, but in reality, you would have something closer to $70,000. That is a sizeable difference in value! There is no way to grow without keeping your money moving. Remember it is a currency; it needs to move.

---

**GREAT QUESTION: AM I FOCUSED ON THE LONG-TERM STRENGTH OF MY MONEY?**

---

# The Cons of Owning Promissory Notes

With as many positives as there are to investing in promissory notes, there are still a few less than stellar points I want to address regarding them. These cons may not hold as much as weight as the pros of owning debt, but it would be irresponsible to neglect to discuss both sides of the coin.

1. **Eventual End Date**

   As great as the passive income of debt income is, the downside is that there is a maturity date on the note. This is the date on which the principal owed must be repaid, and at that point the note is retired, and the monthly income will end. Of course, you can reinvest the money you receive in another promissory note at that point and begin receiving monthly payments from it, but market conditions may have changed by then. You may not be able to earn as much interest as you had been if interest rates are lower than they had been.

2. **Tax Benefits**

   "Well, wait a second Todd, you just listed this as an upside to investing in promissory notes." It's true. I did. The problem is that you have to determine whether the tax benefit associated with holding a promissory note outweighs the tax benefits—mainly the depreciation and maintenance expense write-offs--of owning the real estate. And that will depend on your current tax situation. You can use depreciation and maintenance write-offs to offset income and reduce your tax liability. A tax professional is best equipped to help you decide—and you should absolutely have one on your team. So, there are tax benefits associated with holding promissory notes as opposed to maintaining an investment in the real property securing those notes, but they may be outweighed by the tax benefits of owning the real estate itself. It is up to you and your team to determine which option is best for you.

3. **Regulations and Systems**

   When using promissory notes to finance the sale of property you own, you need to be aware of the applicable laws, regulations, and restrictions to avoid being charged with predatory lending. Now, will you need to really worry about this if you are acting in a transparent and ethical way? No, but it's important that you spend some time with a real estate attorney to ensure that you are abiding by all state and federal laws and regulations, which, by the way, are constantly changing. Staying up to date is the responsible thing to do. As an example, the Dodd-Frank Act restricted the number of properties you can sell to owner-occupants on terms (promissory notes) without employing the services of a registered mortgage lending officer. These laws have been modified a handful of times already and will undoubtedly be revisited in the future. Bottom line: before acting, it is always smart to consult a local real estate attorney and put a plan together to ensure you are acting in accordance with current laws.

   In addition to other systems within your business, you will need to create systems that enable you effortlessly to receive, track and file payments received on your promissory note investments, not only for your own tax purposes, but also for your borrower's purposes. Your borrowers also enjoy tax benefits, and if you don't have systems in place to keep track of principal repayments, interest paid, remaining principal balance, etc., things can get messy and disorganized. There are specific software programs that you can buy to assist with this. There are also companies that specialize in handling these types of transactions. I recommend creating a plan and a system before acting on any investment.

**GREAT QUESTION: AM I DOING THE PROPER DUE DILIGENCE TO PROTECT MYSELF AND MY BORROWERS?**

# Owning Rental Property and Sending Families to Work for You

I am going to teach you the business of owning rental property, but I first want you to think about the next statement very carefully: what if you could send an unlimited amount of families to work for you and your family every single day so you could live the life that you want? What would your life look like? This is the direction I want your mind to take when considering the business of owning assets and owning rental property. At its simplest level, owning rental property is providing safe, affordable, clean, and reliable living spaces for families who are willing to wake up and go to work for you and your family in exchange. If you own one rental property, you will have one person or one family who goes to work every day to make your life and future better. If you own 100 rental properties, you will have 100 families who go to work every morning, for 8 to 10 hours a day, to pay for the lifestyle that you want. That sounds like a pretty good trade to me!

There are literally unlimited ways in which you can acquire and control property so that you can profit from your investment and build long-term wealth and freedom. I will be focusing on owning single family rental properties at this point. I want to work with you to build a strong foundation so that no matter the economic situation, the other market conditions, or the surprises that arise, you will be secure in your mindset and in your ownership practices.

When we think about sending other families to work for us, we need to be aware of the importance of making each relationship win-win. Too often, landlords view renters or tenants as "lesser," as if the tenant owes them something even when they aren't doing a great job of keeping up their end of the bargain. The relationship between tenant and owner is twofold. The owner's job is to provide quality property that is clean and well-kept at a reasonable price, given the specific market. It is the job of the owner to take care of the major maintenance issues and to do so in a manner that is professional and timely. It always amazes me when maintenance on a rental property is neglected, with the owner failing to recognize how it is only affecting the long-term growth of his asset and his family's freedom. Property owners often think short-term as well and worry about the quick $500 expense and not the $1,000 gain from it down the road. The job of the tenants is to love their family, go to work, take good care of the property, and pay their bills on time. This is how simple the relationship should be.

When both parties are honest and trustworthy, the relationship is typically smooth and strong. As property owners, we need to realize that the only thing that makes our properties assets and not liabilities is our tenants! Tenants are our partners in this business. Remember to treat them as such. It is also important to remember this in different economic situations. "There are great people at every income level." I was taught that very early on and it changed my trajectory in life. I stopped praying for my own success and began praying for the success of my customers.

You will notice a pattern in the properties that you own when you begin to grow your portfolio. You will find that when proper expectations are set and the roles of each party are handled correctly, you will enjoy long-term customers (tenants) who want to work with you and only you. This is how your portfolio will grow over time. We will discuss this in more detail later in this book. I will teach you how to take care of others so that they take care of you!

---

**GREAT QUESTION: IS IT BETTER FOR ME TO GO TO WORK BY MYSELF EVERYDAY OR TO SEND 100 OTHER FAMILIES TO GO TO WORK FOR ME?**

---

# The Upside to Owning Rental Property

Much like owning promissory notes, owning rental property is, in my opinion, the single greatest investment you can make in your lifetime. There is no shortage of wealthy people who invest in real estate, and it is the number one asset of millionaires. Investing wisely in real estate has the ability to set you free and set you up for generational wealth. There is no limit on how much you can own, and there is no limit on the amount of money you can invest in it, unlike other traditional "retirement plans."

Real estate has limitless options as well. You can use your capital or someone else's to purchase property, pay down debts, and ultimately own and control an asset. Let's cover some of the most important benefits of owning rental property.

1. **Consistent Monthly Income**

    Real estate has the ability to be one of the most powerful repeat income sources in your arsenal of assets. When the relationship between tenant and owner is handled correctly (whether there is management in the middle or not), the asset has the ability to pay the owner for the rest of his or her life and beyond. This consistent income becomes a basis for further growth and accumulation. The most difficult property to get is the first. That property's consistent flow of income helps you purchase the second, both mentally and financially. The second becomes a third. The third a fourth, and so on. It is important to realize that we are looking to scale this consistent income right off the bat as well. We want to keep in mind that we need to have a team in place and a management system set up so that we aren't trapped inside of our rental business. Good management becomes an extension of the owner and passes on his or her core beliefs. The management should have the best interest of both the owner and tenant in mind so that the relationship stays win-win. If management is solely focused on dollar bills, the business will suffer because poor tenants will be placed and short-term thinking will crush any long-term growth potential.

2. **Possible Appreciation**

So, what exactly is appreciation? Appreciation is another example of supply and demand. Many think real estate always goes up in value; clearly, that isn't the truth. There are always scenarios in which property values can drop. This is why I list this benefit as *possible* appreciation. There are actually two financial factors at work here. One is supply and demand. As long as the economy is strong and the housing supply is less than the demand for it, then we will observe what we call appreciation, wherein the property becomes "more valuable" and sells for a higher price. Thus, we can profit from the sale of the property that we had purchased previously for a lesser amount of money.

The second factor that plays into our ability to profit from the sale is inflation. Inflation is, once again, a general increase in price levels. This means that it takes more dollars to purchase the same item--in this case, property. So, in the end, we may be able to sell a property for more money than we paid for it simply by owning the property and maintaining it for a certain period of time. I look at possible appreciation as a bonus. I focus on the cashflow of the business of the property, and any appreciation is icing on the cake.

3. **Ability to pull from the pond as the pond grows**

There are very few investments that we can make, pull income from monthly, and still see our investment pool of funds grow. Consider a traditional 401k retirement plan A 401k retirement plan is an employer-sponsored, tax-deferred, defined contribution

## IF YOU CAN'T CASHFLOW AFTER THIS

plan. "Defined contribution" means that the amount the employee contributes to the plan is defined. In many instances, the employer may match part or all of the employee's contribution. The contributions are typically invested in stocks, bonds, and mutual funds that rise and fall with the strength of the market. The money must be left in the pool until the contributor reaches a certain age. Otherwise, the contributor gets hit with a heavy penalty tax. Upon retirement, you can begin to pull a monthly salary of sorts from the pool of money that you have acquired over time by saving into this 401k plan.

Now recall the pond analogy I used in the beginning of this book. You pull from that 401k pond every month. The pond has no streams running into it. What do you think will happen to that pond with the passage of time? It will dry up! So, while you pull from this pond, it isn't growing. It is shrinking and withering away. What if you run out? That sounds risky…

Now contrast real estate investments with that 401k plan. You can put the same amount of money into real estate over time. The only difference is that you can pull from this pond, even on the day that you created it. You can pull from this pond for years and years before ever retiring in the form of rental income and/or interest on your promissory notes. Furthermore, you can continue to pull from it every month after retirement, and in the end, the pond continues to grow due to appreciation, rental increases, and inflation. Real estate has streams coming into it! You can pull from real estate holdings infinitely, and as long as the asset is maintained and rented, it will continue to provide you income without diminishing your original investment, barring any outside disruptions. Real estate is also not at the mercy of economic hardships the same way traditional 401K retirement plans are. Always focus on streams flowing into your pond!

Would you rather have a pond that dries up in a short amount of time after pulling from it month to month at retirement age, or would you rather have a pond that provides for you day one and grows larger as you grow older? I have a feeling you would rather have the latter.

4. **Tax Benefits**

   Much like the promissory notes, real estate holdings create even more options for limiting tax liabilities and risk. As previously mentioned, passive and repeat income is taxed at a lower rate than earned income. Real estate holdings give you the ability to write off depreciation. Once again you want to have a certified tax professional on your team to advise you on the best plan of attack. Depreciation can be a powerful tool to use for offsetting rental income. It gives the ability to maximize your tax savings and stretch your dollar further in every aspect.

5. **Fight Inflation**

   Rental properties provide a hedge against inflation since rental rates increase with inflation, and sometimes even more than inflation. In inflationary times tenants have to pay more to rent the same space, so the owner is able to ensure his investment is always working and growing.

6. **Compounding Growth**

   When you own real estate, each new unit you own stacks on top of the last, creating consistent growth in both your income stream and asset base (unless you sell some units along the way). As appreciation, inflation, rental increases, and portfolio growth occurs, your net worth and financial freedom skyrocket. Once you buy a unit, it can be owned forever and build the freedom for your generations that follow.

7. **Leverage and liquidity**

   Many people see real estate as illiquid, but in reality it has more options than almost any other investment on the planet. You have the ability to pull equity out for other investments. You have the ability to secure promissory notes to properties. You have the ability to leverage one property to buy some other item or investment. Real estate can be used as collateral. The best part about all of these options is that, if employed correctly, the property is still yours and will continue to pay you every month while providing you new opportunities to purchase other items or investments. How many other investments can you name that have that ability? I'm not saying there aren't any, but there are few that provide you with this much control and flexibility.

Real estate even has the ability to provide tax-free income if used responsibly and correctly. As an example, assume you purchase a property at a discount due to maintenance issues. You fix those issues, which increases the property's income. The amount of equity you have in the property is measured by subtracting the amount of money you owe from the new value of the property. As an example, suppose you owe $50,000, and property is worth $75,000. Your equity is $25,000.

With $25,000 in equity, you can approach a lender about refinancing the property. The bank will lend you a percentage of the value of the property, and anything above what you owe goes directly into your pocket, tax free. It is tax free because it is technically a loan to you, not profit, which would be subject to taxation. You would, of course, now owe this amount to that bank with interest, but this gives you the ability to leverage that capital into more investments. I would recommend doing this only if the first property—the one against which you borrowed the money for the tax-free payday--alone generates enough income to pay off this loan. If the income from the property cannot cover this new loan payment, don't do it. You will become overleveraged and risk the financial wellbeing of your business. Your asset will have effectively become a liability just so that you could put a small lump sum in your pocket. Do this repeatedly, and you won't be in business long.

---

**GREAT QUESTION: AM I LOOKING AT ALL THE DIFFERENT BENEFITS OF HOLDING REAL ESTATE AND LEVERAGING RESPONSIBLY?**

---

# The Downside to Owning Rental Property

The best part about the downsides of owning rental property is that much of it can be avoided with minimum energy and worry when you have the correct systems and mindset in place. Understanding that there will be problems at times and that there are solutions to each and all of these problems will help in the long run. It is important to note that you will hear different opinions about holding real estate and owning rental property, but, in the end, each person's experiences and results vary in direct correlation to the owner's ability to persevere and problem solve. The better the owner is at establishing win-win situations with the properties for both him/herself and the tenants, the better the experience for everyone involved.

1. **Systems and Management**

    It is important to consider the scale of your rental portfolio at the outset. I have seen a lot of good investors find themselves in trouble because they failed to plan for managing and systematizing their portfolio of properties until it was too late. Then the task of maintaining and keeping up with their properties became overwhelming. Luckily, this problem is easily handled through team-building and outsourcing. You can build your own team through your network, or you can outsource the management of property to third-party companies. It is definitely best practice to interview multiple companies when contemplating outsourcing because you need to ensure that the management company fits all of your core values. Notice I said ALL of your core values, and not just some. If someone is going to be representing you, you want that person to be a projection of you and your values. This will help keep the business running smoothly.

When you purchase your first rental property, don't be afraid to start building that management team right away. Your team may start out small, but you will get great practice at team-building that will be invaluable when you have multiple properties and possibly larger buildings that take more manpower.

2. **Maintenance and Upkeep**

I want you to realize a very real fact: everything around you is deteriorating. Everything. The walls around you, the paint, the flooring, the ceiling, the life of fixtures, all of it. Once you realize that the best shape the property will be in before needing maintenance is the day you buy the property, you will be better able to shift your mindset to focus on quality property and provide top-notch maintenance. Spending on maintenance should be viewed as more of an investment as opposed to just an expense. Attending to repairs and other maintenance items will bring you the best tenants and keep those tenants happy for a longer amount of time, resulting in a more profitable business. Look for value, not just the biggest discount.

Think about the first property you either bought or are going to buy. Think about it needing some maintenance after a few months. Now think about owning 50 to 100 of those properties. What does your life look like at that point? If you have no plan in place, or if you are completely caught off guard by maintenance issues, that question is probably causing you some stress. When you reset your mind to prepare to invest in maintenance, you will realize that this is what the depreciation tax write-off covers, and it is what will increase the value of your properties over time, which, in turn, increases your net worth and cashflow.

3. **Capital requirements**

No matter what anyone says, real estate can be a capital-heavy game. Houses are expensive. Fixing them can be expensive, especially if you use experienced experts for both labor and materials purchases. It can be expensive to hire. It can be expensive and may require even more capital during difficult weather and extreme conditions. Real estate can be expensive to insure and expensive to maintain at times, but it will pay you back 10 times what you put into it if managed correctly. You should always budget for maintenance and updates throughout the time you own the property so that it will continue to grow for you.

When I see people shy away from real estate, it is typically because they are afraid of either the maintenance involved in ownership or because of the capital requirements. Let me say here that the problems that you hear about regarding real estate aren't real problems. They are perceived issues. "I don't want to deal with a leaky toilet at 3 a.m." Perfect, because you probably won't have to, and even if you do, it will happen so rarely that either your management team or an outside contractor will be handling it. Real problems involving real estate are beyond the simple maintenance that generally causes people to be concerned about investing in it.

When people worry about the capital requirements involved in real estate investments, they typically think only of their own personal resources. They don't seem to stop and consider offering others opportunities to invest with them. These others can share their capital to make an investment great. You don't have to use your own money or credit to purchase property.

There is a reason banks and private lenders love property so much. It is consistent and tangible. Everyone will always need a place to stay, and people will generally pay for where they live first so that they aren't out on the street. This great combination makes it easier to secure capital that will grow over a long period of time. Invite others you trust in with you. Always be a responsible borrower and ensure that each asset can stand on its own so that you're not robbing Peter to pay Paul, and when you do, real estate is a great wealth-sharing opportunity.

---

**GREAT QUESTION: AM I FOCUSING ON BUILDING SYSTEMS AND ORGANIZING A TEAM WHILE I AM STILL A SMALL OPERATION SO THAT MY TEAM CAN GROW ALONGSIDE ME AT A QUICKER PACE?**

---

# The "Real Life Cell" on a Spreadsheet is Missing

You may be wondering why a section within a book would ever be named this. I guarantee that you will understand what I mean by the end of my next story.

There are times in life where everything on paper just isn't what it seems. Unfortunately, I watch people every day act blindly on investments and business that only looks good on paper. There are endless examples of things that look good on paper, but just don't seem to perform as it seems they should in real life. Think about how certain sports teams, stacked with talent and experience beyond anyone's comprehension, get beat by the underdog; or the times that certain high horsepower cars get beat by cars with less power because the less-muscled vehicle happens to perform better or have a better driver. These are just a couple examples of how things can look great on paper but, when played out in the real world, don't seem to meet expectations. My point is that it is dangerous for you to buy property based strictly on what it looks like on paper. That is a practice that will send you home broken before you realize how to fix it.

My close friends and I call people who live and die by spreadsheet investing "Spreadsheet Warriors." The problem with spreadsheet warriors is that they typically don't understand what the actual business of real estate is, or what it takes to be successful. They see a property has this many units, that they each should rent for this amount, so, therefore, their income each month will be this great big number, when, in reality, there is a lot of work involved in getting a property to a point in which it could ever reach top-producing numbers.

When I refer to spreadsheets, I am referring to the data that is collected on a possible investment. They are commonly filled in with numbers that "should" be right and are rarely, if ever, exact. Real estate is never exact, due to constantly changing factors, including taxes, maintenance, appraisals, opinions, damages, improvements, labor, etc. It is impossible to look at a property and know to the exact penny what it will bring in year to year and how much it will cost year to year. You always need to budget for outside factors and potential failures. How much you should budget for each situation is really dependent upon your assessment and the property, but I always recommend that people have cash reserves in case of unexpected expenses.

When people fill out a spreadsheet and input income and expenses using a set formula, they are missing the unseen business costs. For example, what if their debt liability is covered only if the property is full 90% of the time? In such a case, what happens if there is a serious unforeseen problem with the property that results in vacancies, leaving the building completely empty for months on end? What do you do now? How do you pay your bills? How do you continue living your life? How do you build a business with no income? These are the missing entries on the profit and loss spreadsheet that is all too commonly accepted as precisely accurate. Spreadsheets are much better at looking back than at trying to predict the future. This said, spreadsheets can be great for estimating potential profits and possible opportunities, but they need to be created judiciously and studied with a jaundiced eye.

Let me share with you a story about a property that I bought and still own to this day. I will explain how I purchased the property, the game plan, the execution, the costs endured, the timeline, and the surprises that I got. As you read my story, I want you to ask yourself what you would have done in my situation and if you would have survived financially if it happened to be your first rental property. I have had more people than not tell me that they would have folded and been out of real estate if this had happened to them. Below, in detail, is one of the most bizarre and information-packed experiences I've ever had In my real estate investing career.

In January 2018, I purchased a property in northeast Ohio where the market is extremely diverse. You can buy a house for a million dollars in exclusive developments, or you can buy houses for merely hundreds of dollars near the inner city. I purchased a one bedroom, one bath, single-family, ranch-style (single floor) home for $15,000. The house, built in the 1950s, had a full, unfinished basement. At roughly 800 square feet, it was a perfect fit for me. This is the type of home that I like to purchase and hold in my portfolio. It had great bones, with a solid foundation, a new metal roof, new windows, a newer furnace, and a brand-new water tank, but the house needed a complete cosmetic rehab. The floors needed torn out; the walls needed patched, smoothed, painted; and both the bathroom and kitchen needed to be renovated. Houses in the area of similar size typically sell in the $30,000 to $40,000 range, depending on condition and lot size. So, on paper, it looked like a great buy. Luckily for me, I understood the importance of budgeting for possible surprises and issues.

The renovation began shortly after closing, and I knew I wanted to put a few dollars away for renovations so I actually borrowed $20,000 from a private investor and designed a promissory note with him with terms of 12%, interest-only. This meant I owed him $200 per month until I decided to pay off that debt. I chose to do this because I had cash reserves set aside for renovations on the property, and I wanted to keep those intact in case of any surprises on this project. I also used the property as security for the debt so my investor was protected against any major loss, including my failure to pay for whatever possible reason. He now has security in owning this property if I failed to pay that has 50% equity in it. Great play for the investor! Win-win.

My game plan was to have the property renovated in the first 60 days and then begin the process for approving the property for our local Section 8 program. The Section 8 program in this specific market is called AMHA, **A**kron **M**etropolitan **H**ousing **A**uthority. We employ Section 8 on our inner-city rentals because the program provides a lot of great people, who would otherwise be unable, the opportunity to rent. Many markets have Section 8 opportunities, but AMHA is especially great. They have a very intensive and specific intake system so it really provides only the best-of-the-best possible tenants--people with clean records--the opportunity for rental assistance. AMHA is also strict on property requirements and mandates that tenants keep their living spaces clean, so it's a great win for us as property owners as well because all of our properties are the nicest in the area. This gives us the ability to get top-tier rental rates, which provides better cashflow for us!

After renovation and AMHA approval, the plan was to have the property rented at $650 per month. This would provide both myself and the private investor repeat cash flow and would provide a great tenant a great property. After 60 days, the property was near completion, and we began the process of approving and renting the property.

At the conclusion of the renovation, I had roughly $8,000 invested in cleaning up the property and labor costs. On top of these expenses, I had also been paying utilities and taxes. These expenses were all factored in when I purchased the property. So far so good, and everything was running smoothly.

During our intake process, we interviewed and declined multiple potential tenants, and even declined a deal that offered a full year of rent upfront… "in cash." This was because we weren't looking for lump sum payments. We weren't even looking for money at this point. We were looking for the best possible person to put in our property so that we could enjoy a long, flourishing partnership. As a side note, don't be the landlord who accepts cash. This is asking for trouble and issues on down the road. Remember the property is our asset, and our goal is to keep it as nice as possible at all times. Cash payments attract the wrong tenants and create accounting issues as well. It is tempting, but don't do it. I provide a detailed discussion about what you need to be aware of regarding the intake process of renting property along with a step-by-step guide later in this book, so keep an eye out for it.

After about 45 days, we accepted someone whom we considered to be a top-tier tenant. Good credit and background history, respectful, and honestly excited to be living in the property. Perfect fit! We signed the documents and prepared to run the paperwork through the approval and inspection process. At this point we had $23,000 invested in the house. It is clean, ready for a tenant, and under market value by roughly $10,000. Not a bad investment so far!

Prior to the AMHA inspection, we had some bad weather and discovered a problem with the installation of the new metal roof. There was a small leak in one corner. No worries; this was covered in our budget. We made the appropriate adjustments and continued forward. Immediately following this, an animal found its way into the attic and began digging holes in the insulation, which resulted in holes in the ceiling in different parts of the house. Again, no worries. These things happen. We sent out the right people to handle the issue, and the problems were resolved. A few days later, someone who lived next door to this house called me to tell me that a tree in his yard, damaged by another storm that hit the area, had partially fallen and a few of the branches had landed on the roof of the detached garage on my property. I sent someone over to inspect the situation, and it was discovered that the branches had not only landed on the roof, but had crashed through the roof! At this point things are slightly more stressful, but overall still not a real problem in the real estate world. I dispatched someone to do the repairs, and the branches were removed—for a "surprise" couple thousand dollars in materials, labor, and expenses.

After all the problems were resolved, the AMHA inspection took place. The house passed inspection after we added a handrail to the five basement steps, and we were set to have our tenant sign the lease and move in. We set up a date for the lease signing with the incoming tenant and the AMHA office. At this point about another 30 days had passed, so this property was purchased in January, completed in early April, and then marketed and finally inspected in June. You can see how the timeline involving a real estate transaction can be at the mercy of different factors and systems, depending on your investment plan. At this point I had paid six months of interest to my private lender at $200 per month, in addition to utilities, labor, materials, and other expenses. I now had approximately $25,000 invested in the property. Still a great investment in which I had equity and from which I would soon get cashflow!

Fast forward a few days, and we have set a move-in date for our tenant. She is ready. We are ready. The property is ready. Everyone is looking forward to working together. In the tenant's excitement, she decided to drive her friend past her new house to show her where she would be living. She wasn't planning on going inside, just driving by. This was a Friday night, right after July 4$^{th}$, and she was due to move in on Monday. It's at this point that the "real life" cell on a spreadsheet would become extremely valuable.

The tenant sent me a text message. She was aware that at this point she would be dealing directly with my management team, but it was okay because we had spoken a handful of times previously, and, to be honest, she's just the kind of person who always puts on a smile, so it was always pleasant speaking with her. She tells me that there is some trash and other belongings in the front yard and that she was concerned. I let her know that wasn't supposed to be the case and that we would send someone over right away to clean up the mess. We assumed that since the entire street knew the house was still going to be vacant until the following week, they decided to have their 4$^{th}$ of July fun in our front yard and had failed to clean up after themselves. It just so happened that my acquisitions manager and I had been putting some systems together and spending time together, so we decided to hop in the car and drive over to inspect the scene ourselves.

We arrived at the property at around 9 p.m., and my eyes focused on the front yard as we approached the house. There was definitely trash as well as some random items along the road, and the nearer we got to the house, the more trash we saw. That's when I looked up and saw the front door wide open, with a man standing in the doorway. *Well, that's certainly not right…* By the time I fully realized what was going on, I felt the car stop, and my manager was opening his door, apparently ready to go full Rambo on these people. I stopped him as quickly as I could and had him drive around the block while I called the police to report a breaking and entering. This is a good lesson to remember: when you are unpleasantly surprised by the unexpected as we were in this case, it's incredibly important to practice your self-awareness and emotional intelligence. You must keep a level head in these situations. You have no idea who these people are or what they are capable of doing.

The police arrived while we were parked down the street, and they approached the house before us. After a few moments they waved us up to speak to three people who were occupying the house. When we went into the house, we realized that these people not only had entered the house, they had moved in! We officially had squatters. The squatters' story was that they had rented the house from someone and that they had paid cash. So, if they are telling the truth, I am on the backend of a rental scam that is popular on Craigslist. At this point I have a $25,000 investment that could really blow up in our faces if we can't get this issue resolved calmly.

# IF YOU CAN'T CASHFLOW AFTER THIS

Let me give you a quick lesson on squatters: these are people who move into a house with their belongings and claim the property as their own. Believe it or not, the laws protect these people. They have what is known as squatter rights. The case becomes a civil case, and the police have zero authority to do anything about it whatsoever. Your only recourse is to evict these people through the appropriate court system, and that typically takes 45 to 60 days. The laws are incredibly biased towards the "tenant," and the owner has very limited opportunity to protect his or her property. You can imagine how stressful this can become in a very short amount of time. I offer specific steps to take to protect your property and assets later in the intake and processes sections of this book.

Now to return to my story: The squatters were clearly not completely coherent. There were some pretty obvious signs of drug abuse, so we decided to tell them that we would return in the morning to discuss how we would resolve this issue. They agreed and gave us and the police all of their contact information, including the places where they worked and the hours that they worked.

We returned the next morning and talked about resolving the situation in a timely manner. I let them know that I felt for them and their situation and that if someone scammed them, then that person was in the wrong and not them. Then I offered them the full $700 that they claimed to have paid, a moving truck to transport their belongings, and two days in a hotel so that we could contact other property owners for referrals and find them a property. Sounds like a pretty solid deal, right?

The squatters verbally agreed, and I left to get a moving truck to begin the process of moving them out before any damage to the property was done so that we could get our tenant moved in. I returned with the moving truck, but when I reached the front door, I found that they had changed the locks on the door while I was gone. They had obviously changed their minds.

For the next 36 hours we negotiated back and forth while the moving truck sat in the front yard. By this time, the police had returned to the property multiple times as well because the squatters had started causing issues at night with the neighbors. It was getting dangerously close to becoming an eviction situation wherein these squatters would remain in control of the property for 45 to 60 days. I had learned more about the squatter personally at this point, so in an effort to avoid the eviction scenario, I made a final offer to her. She had, mind you, moved in two friends, three small children, and two pit bulls with her. Great combination of tenants for anyone who hopes to keep a new property in top shape, right? Remember this was a one bed, one bath house! I had six people living in an 800 square foot, one-bedroom house. My final offer was $1,000 in cash; transportation to a storage unit for her belongings; a hotel for everyone for a week; and a recommendation to a landlord for a new property. I also agreed that I wouldn't pursue breaking and entering charges or report her to child protective services for having three small children in a squatter house, along with unsavory characters and, most likely, drugs.

I told her I would keep my end of the bargain immediately after my team had helped them move out. I also let her know that if she declined my offer, I would give her no money; I would call child protective services; I would pursue breaking and entering charges and request that a court garnish her wages; and I would not recommend her to a landlord. I told her I would also report her to the prosecutor's office so that they could determine if this was a pattern of hers and create a case file on her. I made this final offer in front of a police officer, who told her that he had never before seen property owner extend a helping hand like I was. Her exact response was as follows. "You're going to have to evict me."

Her friends actually yelled at her for declining the offer and went inside. I immediately called my attorney and began the eviction process. The required three-day notice was posted on the door without delay. The court hearing was filed, and thus began the process. Our court date was four weeks later. During this period, the police were called on the squatters no less than 12 times by neighbors. They had reportedly broken into neighboring garages and turned the property into a drug house. Pleasant, isn't it? It gets better!

There were multiple noise complaints, and during one inspection of the property, chickens were found inside the house. So, we now have three adults, three small children, two pit bulls, and… chickens. All inside of a one-bedroom, one-bath, single-floor home. Let's add to the fun. On top of all of this, the squatters worked at a tire shop and began bringing tires home and storing them inside the house. Not outside or in the garage--inside the house. This had now become one of the most bizarre situations I had ever experienced. It honestly became comical at one point.

The shame in all of it was that they were offered help and didn't know how to receive it. That's sad in the end. When I thought about it, I realized how blessed I was to have this type of problem. The problem I had was that I owned nice property that people want to live in, but can't afford, and after 60 or so days, I would still own the property, while they would have to continue searching. It can be difficult to see the light in a situation like this, but I am incredibly grateful for the opportunity to have this type of problem.

Fast forward to about the 45-day mark in this adventure. Our eviction court hearing date is finally upon us. If you have never attended an eviction hearing, it is honestly very simple. The only people involved are you (the owner), the tenant, and the judge, and the whole procedure lasts only a couple of minutes. You may also have an attorney, which I highly recommend, and the tenant may have someone there to represent them. Typically, the tenant doesn't even show up because he (or she) knows that if he hasn't been paying rent, he doesn't have any kind of a case.

Eviction hearings take place in the small claims civil court of the jurisdiction in which the property is located. You would be amazed at how many evictions are scheduled each hour. There are commonly 10 to 20 evictions scheduled each hour in our small claims court. This number will vary depending on the area and the population, of course. I'm telling you this so that if you find yourself in this situation, you will know you are not alone. Evictions are common occurrences. These small claims court judges are constantly handling these cases, so try to be patient with them and trust the legal system. I should also mention that the decision rendered in an eviction hearing will be either to evict or reschedule the hearing. There will be separate hearings for claims of damages, theft, or other illegal activities allegedly engaged in by either party.

Our hearing was quick and to the point. The judge awarded us the right to take the property back, so the next step was to schedule the actual eviction with the bailiff. This generally takes between 8 and 15 days. In our case it took about 12 days. So, if you have been doing the math, these people had managed to squeak out a free place to live for two months at this point.

Up until the eviction date, things were relatively quiet and went as planned. My team was preparing to open the property to the police if need be, secure the property, remove any belongings, and begin renovation once again, since we assumed the property had been badly damaged by the squatters. On the day of the eviction, my acquisitions manager went to the property and found the tenants fleeing the property in a stressed scurry. Not far behind were the police and the rest of my team.

My team opened the door to a most unpleasant surprise. The entire house was being flooded! We joke that we found the third and final wet bandit from the *Home Alone* movie series because the situation seemed straight out of the movies. Wash cloths plugged drains; vent covers had been pulled out to flood the mechanicals; and the plumbing in the kitchen had been removed, while the water tank had been cranked up to do as much damage as possible. We were able to turn off the water quickly after entering the property, but the damage had been done. The entire house had been flooded and destroyed. So, we did the only thing we could do at the time; we started fixing everything so that our original tenant could move in as quickly as possible because, when all was said and done, she was the one who was affected most. She had placed her notice, cancelled her storage unit, and had begun the moving process when this all began two months prior! Our main focus became taking care of this new long-term customer, who would be around for a long time. This may be the most important lesson to take from this: you can't build a business if no one ever sticks by you.

In the end we had purchased the property for $15,000, plus closing costs. There was roughly $8,000 invested in the house prior to this bizarre set of incidents and over $20,000 in damages created by the squatters, who had turned the house into a small pond and stolen all of the appliances. That's right, the cost to repair the damages was more than the purchase price of the house! Where exactly do you find that on a spreadsheet?

Of course, this was a very rare and extreme situation, but I related my experience here to encourage you always to listen to your gut. You should always take the extra step to secure your investment and realize that just because it looks good on paper doesn't mean that you should make the move on it. Consider the outside forces; consider the possibilities of extended vacancy times and possible damages. If you have a deal that looks good on paper, but the amount of work and effort on the front end doesn't seem to add up, let that be a red flag. If you are contemplating your first property, and you see that the spreadsheet says "go," but that the numbers fail to account for the possibility of having a down month or other problems, and you realize that a single issue could cripple you financially, look at other options. Maybe you can renegotiate the deal so that you can minimize your risk. Your first rental doesn't have to be a life-changing home run. It needs to be a property that provides lessons and eventual income for you and your family.

My story wasn't meant to scare you out of investing in real estate, either. Quite the opposite, actually! I wanted to explain how the eviction process works so that you will know what to expect if ever faced with one. There were also business lessons embedded in the story. Always budget for surprises and possible issues. Granted, in my case, I would basically have had to budget to purchase that property twice before I could expect any cashflow from it, and that's a little extreme. However, I wanted to share this with you to let you know that even a problem as wild as the one described can be solved simply, given time.

Our business is perfectly healthy and still growing. These people could not have done anything to the property that would have put a major chink in our armor. This speaks to the importance of building a great team you can rely on and lean on when things like this happen. Consider finding an attorney who specializes in real estate that you can work with before you "NEED" one. Build relationships with contractors and skilled laborers who can help in tight situations. Start building your hub and management team at the outset instead of waiting until you have so many properties that you are stressed out. Build relationships with the local police officers. Let them know who you are and what you do, and they will help look out for you. Think about the importance of having a great insurance agent. I have the best relationship with my insurance agent! When all of this happened, he reassured me that they would be there to help if anything got out of hand, like it did. Guess who was the first person on the phone offering to help me? That's right, him! This entire story was intended to let you know that anything is possible, and no problem, no matter how bad, will shut down your business. After reading this book you will have the ability and the knowledge to create all of the systems you need to thrive in real estate, no matter what.

## GREAT QUESTION: AM I OKAY ASKING FOR HELP?

# Getting Clarity on Long-Term Financial Freedom

Be honest. Have you ever actually broken down the numbers to see how much you would need to make every month repeatedly to be completely financially free? If you answered no, thank you for being honest. I know some of you may have, and that's great! The overwhelming majority usually just say things like, "I wanna be a millionaire." Well, great, we all do… but how do we actually move towards this goal? We need a mental blueprint and a plan. We need to be crystal clear on our intentions and our disciplines so that we know exactly what moves to make next. Unless we are laser-focused on a well-defined plan, we will fail to move forward each and every day. The last thing we need is to get stuck in a lull and lose multiple days due to confusion and/or unconstructive actions that don't move us in the direction of our stated goals.

When folks break down the actual numbers, most of them find that they will need a few thousand dollars of passive income each month in order to escape the rate race. Not $100,000 a month and millions per year, but just a few thousand dollars a month. This should be great news! It is probably already more attainable than you thought possible, and we haven't even begun yet!

First things first. What makes us, or defines us, as financially free? What does it mean financially to have escaped the rat race? Being financially free means that your monthly passive (or semi-passive) income exceeds your monthly obligations and expenses. For example, let's assume you have $4,500 per month in expenses, and you currently earn $5,500 per month working at your job. This is the definition of the rat race because you have to keep trading your time for the $5,500 per month. Otherwise you risk losing everything since you're responsible for $4,500 in expenses. The worst part about the rat race is that it takes up so much of your time that it can be difficult to carve out time to work on your own business and build your own path.

Now let's use the same numbers, but change the type of income you are earning. You still have $4,500 a month in expenses, but now you earn $5,500 in repeat income from real estate holdings and investments. These investments don't require you to work on them every single day, trading your time for the income they generate. Thus, you are free to spend your time as you wish. The best part about being financially free is that you have the time to scale your business and operations so that you can double, triple, and even increase your income a hundredfold without having to trade any more time for that money. When you are stuck in the rat race, the only thing you can trade for income is time, and there are only 24 hours in a day, as we discussed previously, which creates a built-in ceiling on our income potential.

The next step towards gaining clarity regarding your long-term financial freedom is to sit down and figure out exactly how much you need to earn passively to create more options for yourself. How much do you need to earn each month through investments in order to leave your current job and focus on growing your own business and lifestyle? Take the time to print out bank statements, highlight your expenses, rank their importance, get disciplined and determine a specific amount that you need to make each month. The lower your monthly expenses, the quicker you can achieve financial freedom. I have seen people move from the rat race to financial freedom with a single deal. Gaining clarity on what your number is will help tremendously down the road when you are feeling down or frustrated. It will give you a well-defined and concise goal, enabling you to see it within reach and getting closer every single day.

It's important to write all of these numbers and targets down. Keep these goals in mind as you make your day-to-day decisions. This will create a path for you to follow and provide you with some discipline you may have been lacking previously. If you are focusing on minimizing your expenses and maximizing your repeat income, do you think you will be as prone to impulse purchases that don't move you closer to your ultimate goal? Absolutely not! You will be empowered and obsessed with making this new vision a reality. There is no better feeling!

A powerful tool beyond determining your minimum expenses is to work backwards as well. Consider your numbers and set a target goal for your monthly income. Hold that number in your mind and start working backwards. Begin planning on target profit margins and timelines. For example, if you want your passive income to be $10,000 per month and you have a $500-per-rental unit profit margin target, you know you only need 20 properties before you are financially free. Can you work on 20 properties in the near future? Without question you can! And sometimes you end up with profit margins that are greater than you expect, so it may take even fewer properties. The goal of this exercise is to have so much clarity on what we need to do at all times that we can't help but take the next step towards our goal. Remember, earning income is a skill, so you will get better at it over time. Your first couple of properties may take some time to get a handle on, but you will quickly be off to the races after that, creating your own path and impact on this world.

**GREAT QUESTION: DO I HAVE EXTREME CLARITY ON MY TARGET?**

# Assigning New Income to a Debt to Make it Free

Did you know that you can make everything you currently pay for on a monthly basis free? Sound crazy? It's true! Following is the mindset behind this concept.

We commonly use the term "free" to describe anything we don't have to pay for. If someone buys a gift for you, or if a company gives away a sample product, you got those items for free, right? Well, in reality, nothing is truly free. There is always a cost somewhere in the picture, whether it be a financial cost or a time cost. What if we could make someone else pay for all of it? If you have a $500-per-month payment and that payment was lifted off of your shoulders, how much would that help you? I bet a lot! In this section I am going to teach you the mindset shift behind creating free expenses and freeing up your hard-earned capital to grow.

This is replacing expenses at its finest. I want you to go through your expenses and pick one out that speaks to you the most. It may be the smallest because you feel it's the easiest to replace, or it may be the most painful that causes you stress month to month. Once you pick this expense out, write the amount down and keep it in your mind. It doesn't matter whether the amount is $30 or $3,000. It is the concept and practice that is important. That is what will ultimately release you from the rat race for the long term.

Now that you have a specific expense and the amount thereof in mind, start brainstorming ways to replace that expense with a totally new outside line of income. How can you replace that expense with a new income

## IF YOU CAN'T CASHFLOW AFTER THIS

from real estate? If you have a $400-per-month bill that eats at you every month emotionally, how might you generate an extra $400 every month so that you can eliminate that expense with that extra $400 each month and keep the original $400 that you earned in the bank or working towards an investment. Let me give you a specific example of how I do this with my finances.

My wife wanted a new car. Now, we had the financial ability to go out and buy a new car for her, but if we just went out and bought a new car and financed it through the dealership or the bank, what would happen? Our expenses would increase, while our income stayed the same. That's not good! That's not how you can stay financially free for the long term, so we had to think of a way to replace that expense with new income that we didn't necessarily have to trade time for. To determine the amount needed, we went to the dealership, and my wife picked out the car that she wanted. It was a new white SUV, and with all the options she chose on it, the monthly payment came to $459 per month. The insurance payment on the new car amounted to about $30 a month, so in total, we would have about $489 in new expenses that we would need to replace.

Now, many people would have bought the car and then looked for ways to make up the extra expense with passive income or by working more hours. This isn't how we operate in our household. She envisioned what she wanted and then transferred her vision to real life by test driving the car and determining the expense. Before we could purchase the car, my job was to replace this expense with some sort of passive income so that the new car created no increased financial liability for us. With insurance included, our monthly payments would be $489 for 72 months at 0% interest. I decided the best thing to do would be to create a promissory note with a similar rate and terms so that when we made the purchase, we could immediately use the new promissory note income to pay for the new SUV every month. In the end I sold a piece of property that we had purchased at a discount and fixed up to an end buyer on terms that would pay us $500 per month for 72 months. Someone else just bought our brand-new car for us! The promissory note also has a small amount of interest built into it, so that money can grow over time. If the end buyer were to decide to pay the note off suddenly, we would simply use that money to pay off the car and own it free and clear.

By practicing delayed gratification and discipline, my wife got her brand-new SUV, and our net monthly cashflow never changed. While, actually, we made $11 more per month. When you adopt this mindset with your finances, it is impossible for you to run out of money, barring any outside factors or large sudden changes. When you adopt the practice of creating new income before adding a new expense, you will be able to enjoy the fruits of life while never having to work any harder to get them or losing any money. This is how the rich play the game. You want to play like the rich! This will work at any scale because this is a universal principle and not based solely on money. If I want to buy a Ferrari, I can do so for free by determining the monthly payments and replacing those payments before purchase. I have the ability to assign new income to this new expense, and until the item is resold or paid off, my cashflow doesn't suffer.

The key to success is to always ensure that you take the one extra step to secure long-term income and cashflow. Don't make the mistake of replacing one expense with another on the same line of income. If you have $1,000 per month in car payments and you decide to sell a car or multiple cars for a newer, nicer car, which will require the same monthly payment, consider putting that $1,000 a month you're saving from having sold the original car into an asset that will pay you every month before you buy the new car. This will free up more assets and capital and help you grow beyond your current limits. You can't go broke when you always assign NEW repeat income to expenses. This will ensure your growth over the long haul.

---

**GREAT QUESTION: WHAT CAN I DO TO BEGIN REPLACING EXPENSES WITH NEW LINES OF INCOME SO THAT I CAN ESCAPE THE RAT RACE AND ENSURE MY LONG-TERM FINANCIAL STABILITY?**

---

# Scaling and Team Building

There is one consistent characteristic that people who are more successful in real estate and in business share. They have great people around them! These investors and business owners have discovered how to hire the best people possible to build systems around and strengthen their weaknesses to create a more well-rounded machine. Scale and growth are two important factors that must be kept in mind when making major decisions and implementing new systems. You want to be able to grow your revenues without having your operations grow at the same rate, resulting in more and more overhead.

The inability to outsource and trust others to complete daily tasks limits the amount your real estate portfolio and business can grow. A single person can do only so much in a day, and with any sort of real estate holdings, this time will be soaked up with less important, non-income producing activities very quickly. Outsourcing and investing in others doesn't have to be as scary as it seems. A lot of the concerns about hiring and building reliable teams relates to the fact that there is so much unknown in the beginning. You may have an endless amount of questions regarding where to start, how to hire, who to hire, where to look, and how to best place a new hire in the correct role. I will be going into depth about the process that I use for hiring, transitioning, rewarding, and even firing. It is important to fire! It is crucial for your business and the person being fired as well. You are doing both yourself and the individual who is obviously not thriving in your business a disservice when you don't let them go. Firing someone is one of the most difficult things you will ever have to do, but when it is handled properly, both parties are left better and stronger because of it. I will share some my experiences, both right and wrong.

The principles within this section will teach you the correct approach to use to find new help and build systems that will enable your new hires to thrive so they can become irreplaceable and enjoy truly rewarding careers within your company. Think about your own current situation as you read this section. Think about what you may need to outsource first (or next). If there is any aspect of your business that won't run without your being there, hands on, there is an opportunity for you to outsource a task and a responsibility. It is irresponsible to have a business that can run only with you there. If the business is dependent on your active involvement, your employees and contractors are at risk because if something were to happen to you, then their careers and security would vanish in your absence. We need to build businesses outside of ourselves so that the portfolio continues to thrive and grow without our day-to-day interaction. The ideal scenario is for you to become a consultant within your own business.

Consider the businesses that you have seen lose value or even go bankrupt after losing their founder or visionary. Apple was tanking and had to bring Steve Jobs back. When the mega coffee chain, Starbucks, began to slide, Howard Shultz had to return to the company eight years after vacating the CEO position from 2000 to 2008. Dominos had to bring in J. Patrick Doyle to rejuvenate the failing pizza brand completely and turn around the reputation of the once unstoppable international pizza franchise. When a company's leadership fails to promote the vision of the company through stellar execution, the company begins to fail. It all starts with the leadership (you) and is carried out by your trusted team. With no team, you will have no growth. So how do we build a team that will carry out our vision? Let's talk about it.

The first step in team and system building is to create a business plan, which is simply a document wherein you stipulate the mission and objectives of the business and the strategies you plan to use to achieve them. You would be amazed at how many people start companies or begin investing with the dream of building a multimillion-dollar business and neglect this first step. A business plan gives you a blueprint and a map to follow and gets and keeps you organized. If you lack clarity on exactly what you want to do, you won't have the process to achieve it.

The business plan that you create doesn't necessarily have to be a 50-page, in-depth description. Create a plan in a manner that you believe will work best for you. I personally have generalized plans with plenty of room for adaptation. This way, the more I learn, the more I can implement new strategies without feeling I am going off track. I may come up with a better idea for my business and how to enhance its growth, and I make sure to employ that strategy. Your plan should describe the purpose of your business, what your target goals are for the near future, and the long-term impact you hope to make. Having this base guideline will enable you to recognize the roles and the systems that you will need to bring your plan to life. If your end goal is to own a single rental property, you won't need the operations and manpower that a business with a 1,000-unit portfolio of commercial buildings will need. Match your targets with the impact you want to make in life. This will allow you to create the exact business that you desire and live the fullest life that you choose, not the life that someone else chooses for you.

If you happen to be someone who is more detail oriented and feel better if you have each and every piece spelled out, complete with various scenarios, you should do that. Do what works best for you. If you need more help, just research how to write better business plans, and you will get better at them with practice. The first time will be confusing and uncomfortable, but after a while, you may catch yourself creating one on a Friday night while your friends are trying to get you to focus on them!

The next step in team building and hiring is to decide what needs to be outsourced first. When you first begin your real estate investment company, you will be a one-man or one-woman show. You will be wearing all of the hats of business. You will constantly be switching from role to role: marketing, sales, accounting, customer services, and finance. In the beginning it is essential to learn all of these roles and understand what it takes to thrive in each one. There will be certain ones in which you will be less comfortable and less skilled, and it is important to note these. This will be a sign of what you will need to help your fledgling business grow in the fastest and healthiest way.

When deciding what aspect of your business needs help first, you need to look within yourself. If you have a failing marketing plan and are struggling with lead generation, it will make sense to focus on this piece of your business first. With a poorly executed--or no--lead generation, you will fail to produce any revenue. Understanding yourself and knowing your weaknesses will allow you to design your business from the ground up. If you are great at acquisitions and love dealing with the sellers in your market and have no problem looking at property and building rapport with people, you should be the one filling that role in the business initially. It wouldn't make sense to hire a sales person because you already have a strong sales person. You! You will eventually want to hire a sales team, but not first if that happens to be your strength. Look inside yourself and be honest with yourself. Say aloud, "I am terrible at _____." Whatever that blank is, look to fill that role first.

I often suggest that people hire a personal assistant first. When we're getting started, we may not be great at realizing what does and doesn't work for us. I commonly see students who are either overwhelmed, or disorganized, or both, running from one job to another. Having a personal assistant to help you get organized and handle the non-income producing tasks can free you up to focus on the one most important task that day, whether it be marketing, sales follow-up, contract signing, or closings.

When you hire someone to be your personal assistant, or to fill any other role for that matter, it is important to realize that you are transitioning from performer to delegator. This will take time and practice initially, but building trust in your team and allowing them to make the mistakes that you have made at some point will be part of the process. It is important to realize that your early interaction with them will be key. You need to train this person to act in the most profitable and effective manner that your experience has taught you. What you can't do is hire someone and expect that person to know exactly how you work and exactly how your business operates best. You need to mold them into a trusted team member who can handle the tasks at hand. Being loving, patient, and clear are keys to a thriving relationship and growing efficiencies. With this comes consistency. It is important to be direct and clear so that the communication between you and the team member is fully understood. Poor communication will break down systems quicker than anything else in business.

Your emotional intelligence comes into play here. You must be consistent in your emotions and reactions. It will be very confusing to the team member if you fly off the handle over some issues and remain calm over others. Remember that almost all decisions and mistakes made can usually be reversed, so don't forget to support your team members with this truth. You will be the atmosphere for your team. The team will go as you go. With this in mind, be sure to instill your team with helpful vibrations so that everyone can succeed together. This atmosphere creates a comradery that allows you to be approachable and open, which keeps all lines of communications open. People will stay with your company longer when they feel heard and that they can come to you when there is a problem. Having this open-door policy will keep small problems small, and they won't have the ability to grow, fertilized by fear or stubbornness.

After determining what role you want to outsource, you need to figure out how to match someone to that role so that they will thrive and want to go to work every day. This was one of my biggest struggles when I began outsourcing. When I first started hiring people, I wanted to help the people closest to me. I wanted my friends and family to do better, so I hired them and gave them the opportunity to succeed and make more money. The problem with this strategy was that I wasn't matching people's personalities to the roles I needed filled. I was simply filling roles with folks who had the necessary qualifications or experience. That sounds like it would be a reasonable litmus test for hiring someone, right? Match a person's qualifications and experience to the job at hand. The problem with this approach is that it neglects to consider why they do what they do and what makes them happy.

You see this approach used in job advertisements. The ad typically indicates that the company is looking for someone with five years of experience in whatever field it is, and they list specific qualifications needed, such as being proficient in certain software programs, writing, speaking, etc. This completely drops the ball in that it doesn't match the type of person to the role.

Anyone can learn a new skill. I love it when I hear someone say, "I hired so and so because they had 10 years of experience in this field." Yeah, that's great, but do they hate their life? I garnered many experiences and qualifications when I worked a traditional job that I could list on a job resume and get job offers, but I would never succeed in that field because

I hated doing that kind of work. It just so happened that my first job fell into a certain category, and all my future jobs followed suit. (I know you're wondering what field. It was phone sales. Yuck!) "Todd you have three years' experience on the phones. That's great. I'd love to hire you!" Just writing about it now caused me emotional distress. That's how much I hated being on the phone! To this day, I hate being on the phone. It was one of the first responsibilities that I outsourced to an acquisitions manager. He is great on the phone, and he enjoys it. I might have been very good at it myself, but that doesn't matter because talking on the phone is the bane of my existence. Listen to yourself!

The proper way to match someone to a job is to match who they are as a person to the role. Rather than posting that you are looking for an acquisitions manager with five years of experience on the phone and at least two years' experience in the real estate industry, with good speaking and typing skills, focus your ad on who they are and how they succeed. Consider the difference in the following two ads:

**Ad 1: Looking to hire acquisitions manager.**

- o   Job requirements: 5 years sales experience, 2 years within real estate
- o   Skills required: proficient with software apps, speaking on the phone, strong communication skills
- o   Ability to work 6 days per week
- o   Open to commission-only pay
- o   Owns reliable vehicle to get to and from work

**Ad 2: Looking to hire ambitious, outgoing person who wants to learn as they go!**

"X Investments company" is looking for someone fun to work with and someone who becomes more driven and determined every time he or she hears the word "no!" We would love to hire someone who wants a new experience every day and isn't afraid to work unique hours in order to grow and profit! We look forward to hearing from you if you are someone who can handle a little discomfort and adapt with each new property we look to acquire. Pay is based upon the amount of killer deals that we take down together and the size of the portfolio that we create. The more the merrier!

We are going to be spending a lot of time together, so I'd love to meet up and talk about your goals and see how we can reach them together!

Of these two ads which one do you think will attract the person more likely to thrive within your business? You are very likely to get more responses from the first ad, but it will be littered with people not happy with what they are doing. They look at the specific qualifications of the job because that is the type of work they've always done, without realizing that they can do anything in the world if they just choose to do so. The second ad, on the other hand, will only attract people whose personalities fits the description. These people will be raising their hand to the rare aspects of each point in the ad. These are the people you will want to interview to determine if they are the perfect fit. Didn't that second ad just feel better, too? I want to work at that place! The first ad sounds like the jobs I used to have…

Assume you find someone with the second ad. Their personality fits; they want the job; you like them; and they seem like a great match, but they don't have much, or any, experience in the specific role you're looking to fill. This is where you remember that the human mind is malleable and not fixed. People can learn skills and are much more likely to learn skills quickly and successfully when their personality matches the responsibility. You rarely dislike things that you are good at. Addressing the hiring situation in this fashion will ensure that your hires will like what they are doing and will improve over time. Remember that at one point you never had the skills they are learning, either. Your training ability will come into play here, and it will improve over time as well. Teaching is a skill! Don't be afraid to hire someone driven to learn something new. Invest in your team, and they will pay you dividends forever.

Now that we have a possible team member in our pipeline, we want to move them through to the next step of our hiring process. We need to match their personality to the job role. We need proof that their instincts are a match for their daily tasks and functions. We don't want to put someone who is timid and stubborn in an outside sales role. As I said before, people can learn new skills, but typically their instincts are engrained. If you find you perform better under certain conditions, a personality test or a test that measures your instincts will help you determine why. We want to match that "why" to the responsibilities of the job. I have all my job candidates take two to three different personality tests. One test measures instincts. The other two measure personality type and reactionary tendencies. This allows me to discover the true relationship of the potential candidate to the position for which he or she is applying. You will be able to match someone who thrives in a scenario wherein each day finds them in a different location, meeting new people, to a position that requires that, and someone who needs specific structure and an environment with minimal change to a position that is more suited to that personality type.

If you were to match a personality that is very grounded and needs a similar environment each day, with trusted people they can rely on around them and a specific start and stop time, with a job that requires an outgoing personality and involves travel, constant networking, and possibly meeting people at their own personal properties, do you think that will be a good match that will work out well for you and the employee? No, of course not!

These personality tests will ensure that you match the type of person to the job, which will help your business explode! You won't have to fight constant turnover and frustration. You also have the possibility of more and more employees becoming your linchpins. A linchpin is someone who is irreplaceable. When someone in your business becomes irreplaceable, his or her performance and output help the business grow, and everyone succeeds because of it. When someone gets to this stage in the business, do you think he or she will feel like changing jobs, or will that person prefer to continue to grow and thrive? Linchpins feel like an important piece of the team because they are, and this results in long-term partnerships and relationships.

Now, even with all of the best intake systems and front-end screening, you aren't going to build the perfect system and hire the perfect team members each and every time. Especially on the first try. You need to be aware of when it is time to adjust someone's role or eliminate his or her position with the company all together. There are signs and patterns that you will come to recognize that indicate that something may need to change in the near future.

When you hire someone to work for your company and help build your real estate business, you need to be aware of their qualities that aren't readily replaceable. When someone lacks any skills that are extraordinary for your specific product or service, he or she will be the first person who may cause problems. There will be a lack of purpose and a lack of energy in the performance of that person's specific roles within the business. The people who can be easily replaced tend to ask for more and more in an attempt to fulfill something within themselves. You can't fix this! When someone has an inherent issue, it is not your job to drop what you are doing and try to fix it. This is one of the first signs that you need to remove someone from your business.

The person who needs to be removed might be a money partner who is becoming too expensive because he or she feels irreplaceable, even though money is readily available everywhere, or it might be an operations employee who isn't as dedicated as the rest of the team in supplying the best possible service to your customers. There is zero lack of money in this field. Real estate is one of the most heavily invested-in categories on the planet. So, if you observe your money becoming more expensive, be aware of it and remedy the issue right away. This problem will only grow over time, and the longer it is ignored, the more difficult it is to solve in a quiet manner.

Trusting your gut is important in hiring, but it is even more important in firing. If you have a team member who always seems to cause a problem, even when things are going well, you need to remove that person as quickly as possible. It is only a matter of time before he or she stunts your growth, becomes a menace within your culture, and costs you serious dollars. It will be uncomfortable to confront the person with the issue, but it will be more painful if he or she remains with your company any longer. It will be painful and costly for the business, and it will be painful for the employee as well. This is a relationship that needs to end for each party to continue to grow.

When you need to remove someone, there are some key factors to keep in mind. I have found that when you have a set of principles and processes to handle these situations, it works out best for both the company and the employee. Listening to the person and hearing his or her thoughts has been beneficial to us as we build our systems. This is an emotional time for multiple people, so it needs to be handled in a way that enables each person to be heard and allows the person being let go to feel that he or she will be able to find a better position because of the skill set honed while employed by you.

It is not uncommon for our company to offer someone who is leaving recommendations and referrals for other positions. After all, our goal is to support our community and our team members. We understand that not everyone is going to be a great fit, but that doesn't mean we don't respect them and care about them. If we can help them find a role that will work better for them, we are more than open to doing that, as long as this person was someone who was willing to work with us and put in the effort to be part of our team. This process takes time and practice, but this situation typically is a direct reflection of the quality of the leadership in the company. If there are multiple highly emotional altercations that result in firings or in people quitting, you know you have a management problem.

One rule that we have in our company is that we don't fire or lay off during low cashflow months or struggling financial times. We look at our business as a family, and you wouldn't fire your grandmother because you made less money one month. We all find ways to sacrifice for the common good, and ultimately, we have found that the whole family is stronger and works better together. This has been painful in the past, but has turned out to be a great choice in the long run.

With a growing team and a business focused on scaling, it is easy to lose track of your timeline and your purpose as a company. It is very easy to want to go from $50,000 per year to $10,000,000, but you need to learn how to make $100,000 in a year before you make $1,000,000 or more. It's not to say that there aren't cases where companies and teams grew faster than this, but it is also well documented that growing too fast can cause a number of problems.

If you fail to focus on strong operations and scalability, you will find yourself overrun with issues that will cause your business to suffer. Constant exponential growth will always reveal the weak link in your business. Rather than try to grow as fast as possible, focus on building a strong foundation and decide on what move to make next so that you can be best prepared. If you have never owned a piece of real estate, it may not be wise to buy a 200-unit apartment complex that has deferred maintenance issues and drug rings living inside just because you thought it was a "great deal." A problematic property of that size will quickly highlight the weaknesses within your business. When you have a strong foundation, you become recession proof and have the ability to grow in any market and in any way that you wish. This foundation will create more opportunities for you to capitalize on, and it will create options for your business so that you can adapt and pivot as needed.

When you focus on scalability and the growth of the company over time, you will realize the strength of your foundation and the options that it creates for you. If you have 10 properties in great condition performing month-to-month in a single marketplace, you will have more options than someone who reaches for anything that he or she can grab, hoping to be able to solve the problems inherent in each property. Instead of rushing into "needing" 100 units, consider how much different your life will look with 5 more, 10 more, and then 20 more. By practicing this way of thinking, you will find your groove and be able to put the throttle down when the time comes, with all of your pieces in place. The small deals will help you see where you are vulnerable and need fortification in order to capitalize on the largest opportunities in the country.

---

**GREAT QUESTION: HOW DO I BUILD A STRONG FOUNDATION SO THAT MY TEAM AND I ARE TAKEN CARE OF AND CAN FOCUS ON SCALING THE BUSINESS OVER TIME?**

---

# Wholesaling for Truly Passive Income

Near the end of the first book in this series (*If You Can't Wholesale After This.. I've Got Nothing For You*), I provided a step-by-step process for creating truly passive income through wholesaling. I want to revisit this, but I want to expand on it further by applying what we have just learned. In the first book, you learned that you can take your assignment fees for selling contracts in unique and creative ways so that you get paid hundreds of times instead of just once. This secures a consistently growing monthly income for you without adding any extra time to your wholesaling process. These transactions involve taking a security position with the end buyer in the property by creating a promissory note. A promissory note, in its simplest form, is a written document signed by the involved parties that specifies the agreed-upon terms for the repayment of a debt obligation.

For example: Assume I sell my purchase agreement for a property to an end buyer for $10,000. Instead of simply taking a $10,000 check, the buyer and I agree that he or she will pay me $10,000 over 60 months with 10% interest. This results in a $212.47 monthly payment and a profit of $12,748.23 over time. Structuring the deal in this manner enables you to get paid more over time, and you get paid consistently, which gives you a more constant cashflow. This also helps with difficult tax situations because you aren't getting paid in one lump sum that can trigger a heavy tax liability. There is also the added benefit of having security in the property. You have a right to the property if the buyer fails to pay you as specified in the note. You can foreclose on the buyer if need be, and you will own the property without ever paying a dime for it. These are just a couple of reasons why taking promissory notes in lieu of a lump sum payment can benefit you and your business.

What if we added the practices that we learned in the previous sections? What if we applied outsourcing and hiring reliable team members to help scale this business practice and build a relatively risk-free foundation that spits out consistent cash flow without any operational or managerial responsibilities? We would have the ability to scale the amount of deals that we are doing on a month-to-month basis without creating any more risk until we are ready for it and have a foundation that is built to last. If this sounds like a bank, you have heard right. This is essentially what banks have done. They have built reliable teams that help create and grow wealth by creating more and more passive income through note creation. They build their wealth and foundation by earning more and more interest and picking and choosing the best and most profitable notes to cash in on, while investing in only the most qualified people.

We may be acting in similar ways to banks when focusing on promissory notes and holding lien positions, but the great part about our setup is that we have the ability to grow passive income through wholesaling in other ways, too. We have the ability to sell contracts to other buyers for lump sums. If a buyer has the funding resources, we can choose to do this as well, while banks typically focus on creating lending opportunities. As mentioned previously, many people see wholesaling real estate as a job that always involves more time input, but actually, by employing promissory notes and building a team to handle the time-consuming aspects, you have the ability to separate yourself from the business and create a branch that has endless earning potential without your having to focus on it each and every day.

Building a wholesaling division and a team to handle each step within the process creates payroll options as well. Since wholesaling is primarily fee-based, you can pay your team hourly rates or bonus income, wherein each closing results in a flat payout. Paying based on results creates an energetic culture because each member holds a role and is rewarded by growing the company. You can create scalable pay structures so that the more the company makes, the more the company shares revenues with its team members, whether that revenue comes from closings or other sales.

The goal of this is to create a certain level of hunger within the team. It isn't uncommon for people to get dependent on comfort, so always rewarding better performance helps create a culture wherein the members always want to move forward and grow. Regardless of whether money, recognition, or status is the motivating factor for a specific team member, this type of pay structure has the ability to influence and inspire.

Creativity in incentivizing your team is important as well. Consider monthly rewards for top performing members. Maybe you could reward them with days off or extra bonuses. This will create a buzz and a target to hit so that everyone gets better.

Below is a doable structure of a team that can be a strong branch for creating repeat income from wholesaling, while not breaking the bank. Now, will you hire all of these positions at once when you first start out? No, probably not. Over time you will fill in the blanks and continue to strengthen your team, which, in turn, will free up more and more of your own time. This will allow you to focus on other larger, and more important, business tasks. You will be focused on the direction of the business as opposed to just the day-to-day operations.

Team Members:

1. Acquisitions Manager
2. Marketing Specialist
3. Data Expert
4. Sales Coordinator
5. Personal Assistant
6. Transaction Coordinator
7. Office Manager

Team Member Job Descriptions:

1. Acquisitions Manager - Focuses on securing properties at price points that make sense for the buyers in your network. This person may be paid a salary and/or bonus-style payments. Typically, this

person will be on the ground floor in handling sellers and following up with the marketing team. This person will help create a target market and sales niche.

2. Marketing – Handles all design and distribution of the paid and free marketing campaigns. This person works directly in coordination with the acquisitions manager and data expert so that the marketing campaigns become more refined and targeted over time, creating a high conversion rate. This person can be paid hourly.

3. Data Expert – This role is specific to refining marketing and helping to create higher conversion rates by looking further into the lead generation system. This person designs the targeted lists on which the marketing team can act. The data expert works directly with the marketing team/specialist. This person will also help track conversion rates on marketing and key performance factors, including how much, on average, it costs to get an offer accepted; how many pieces of marketing it takes to get a call back; and the average costs per closing. We pay our data experts by the hour.

4. Sales Coordinator – Main focus is networking and bringing more and more deals to the table by networking with financial partners and marketing any properties that we currently own or contracts that we have for sale that fell through with our original buyers. This person is typically paid on a bonus structure based on company revenue. The sales coordinator interacts with the acquisitions manager and with marketing for feedback.

5. Personal Assistant – This role is filled by a trusted member to handle the daily office tasks and operations that would normally involve the owner (you). This person handles incoming calls, emails, and assists in managerial tasks, such as maintenance and work orders on property you own. This person typically helps handle scheduling and invoices as well as payroll. This person interacts with all aspects of the business. This person can also commonly serve as the office manager. The personal assistant is typically paid hourly.

6. Transaction Coordinator – This person's sole focus is on deal flow and handling transaction processes. This person is in contact with

title companies and does contract follow-up with sellers and buyers. This person handles all title company and closing scheduling and is the point of contact for the buyer, seller, and title companies once a contract has been signed. The person in this position is crucial for setting expectations and running multiple smooth transactions. This person is typically paid hourly.

7. Office Manager- Can be one and the same as the personal assistant, but this position can be filled by a separate person who ensures all day-to-day operations are running smoothly. Office managers typically work with each department, but in close coordination with data experts to help create target sales and action points. This person is typically paid hourly.

It is important to note that each of these departments needs to have open lines of communication with the others for the business to run smoothly. In order for the marketing team to determine which marketing tool is performing best, they must be in contact with data experts. This needs to happen before they scale into a larger marketing campaign. It also stretches every dollar further to create a more profitable business. This type of organization is facilitated by a positive culture and software investments.

Having the proper software to help each member handle different business tasks can mean the difference between scaling and failing. The sales coordinators and acquisitions managers need software to track follow-up calls and appointments, while the marketing team needs to be able to see the results of the performance tracking done by the data experts. The office manager needs to be able to track activity and performance, while the transaction coordinator needs a schedule of future closings and has to know what contracts need attention in order to close.

There are hundreds of software systems available to help teams grow and prosper. If you do a quick online search of CRM (Customer Relation Management) software, you will find one that best fits your current needs and budget. You should be looking for software systems that fit your team best, work well with your systems, and focus on the most important organizational pieces first. A CRM system that facilitates constant organized lead generation is paramount for maintaining high revenue and enabling growth

When you begin the team building and outsourcing process, find team members to combat your weaknesses and dislikes so that you can double down and leverage your best strengths. Hate accounting and scheduling? Work to find a personal assistant first. If you have no issues with organization and task-filling, think about outsourcing lead generation so that you can focus on acquisitions. There is no specific right or wrong answer. Each business is a little bit different.

**GREAT QUESTION: WHO SHOULD I HIRE FIRST IN MY BUSINESS?**

# CASE STUDIES

Before transitioning to our step-by-step guide for structuring deals for cashflow, I want to share a couple case studies with you. These are real deals that I have completed while building my business. I will provide actual descriptions and use real numbers so you can realize the potential you have when you structure your business for repeat income.

# The Hoarder Home

One of the first properties that I sold on terms, using a promissory note to generate monthly income, was a house that had "good bones." The house had a good roof, a solid foundation with a dry basement, and the siding was in good condition. Overall, the outside of the house wasn't in too bad a shape, but the inside was a different story. The house was a hoarder house. The house was packed from floor to ceiling in some areas with everything and anything that you imagine. There wasn't a lot of actual trash in the house, which was good, but the house was jam-packed with items collected over the years, and the family had owned the house for over 70 years!

This particular house was in a city area that is typically more blue-collar, with pockets of lower income. The neighboring houses were well kept, with the exception of one or two, and the houses of similar size in the area were selling in the high twenty to lower thirty thousands. This can be a difficult range to buy in when you want to resell to a traditional buyer who needs to get a bank loan because banks don't typically loan on houses with lower sale values. They don't because they don't earn enough interest on the loan to meet their risk/reward requirements. This creates great opportunities for us because it allows us to offer our homes at higher prices on terms that provide us with a down payment and regular monthly income. This is great for the buyers because they can't get a typical bank loan, and they don't have the wherewithal to pay cash for the house. We get to solve their problem by taking a down payment and accepting monthly payments; we act as the bank for them.

I got this lead from a free Craigslist ad that I had posted, and the family called to hear what I had to offer. We talked about the issues with the house and the clean-up that would be needed, but I asked what the real problem was. It turned out to be family-related; the family had to move into a different style of home due to a health condition. They needed a bathroom on the first floor. We agreed that I would cover the expenses to locate a house that met this requirement and move them into it, as well as the security deposit and first month's rent. In return, I would take ownership of their current home so that I could fix it and resell it. The family agreed, and my total cost came to $2,500. In return for solving their problem, I got the house at a price that I could make work.

Over the next few weeks, I put roughly $7,500 into the house, which included renting multiple dumpsters for the clean-up and remodeling the small kitchen and bathroom. When all was said and done, I had given the house a cosmetic facelift, and the major mechanicals were in good working condition. I had a total of $10,000 invested in a property that the market valued somewhere in the neighborhood of $30,000.

One option for reselling the property would have been to sell it for $30,000 to a cash buyer. Our profit would have been $20,000 before capital gains taxes and closing costs. At the end of the day I would have made roughly $12K to $13K on the deal. Not a bad return on $10,000!

Instead of selling it right away to a cash buyer, I asked myself how I might make this even more valuable and provide a house to someone who might not have the cash in hand to buy it outright, but who could come up with a down payment and eliminate all of my risk in the house.

I chose to ask for $10,000 down, on a selling price of $38,500. This paid for my investment in the property completely. I am cashed out at this point with zero risk. My asking price was above market rate at the time, but my offer of seller financing opened me up to more buyers. Over the next two weeks I showed the house a handful of times and received a full-price offer, which I accepted. The buyer came up with the down payment at closing, and we agreed he would pay just under $500 a month at 6% for 7 years. Counting the interest I earned, I received over $43,000 for a house worth $30,000. I will make closer to $28K to $30K after taxes instead of only $12K -$13K. My profit on this deal exceeded what I had paid for the home originally, and after the down payment, I had creatively created a new line of income out of thin air, while still having the original $10,000 to reinvest in another property. The accounting books would show that I technically lent the buyer nearly $30,000, but, in reality, I never took a dime out of my pocket. Not a bad deal!

When you think about structuring deals like this, think about how they stack on top of each other. That deal pays nearly 100 times instead of just once! How many times can you repeat this process to grow your wealth?

# The Smoker Lounge

As you may have already guessed from the title of this case study, this house had been filled with a family of smokers--for 40 years! If you have never been in a house that has been smoked in continuously, you will learn that nicotine from the cigarettes will actually begin to stick to the walls and ceiling. As you may imagine, it is not the prettiest sight or smell. The great part about a house like this is that very few people will ever consider buying this house. Many investors don't understand the cleaning process for a house like this, and many retail buyers won't look past the smell. Luckily for us, we have worked with similar houses in the past and understand what it takes to remove nicotine stains and the smell of cigarette smoke.

This specific house happened to be a property that the parents had bequeathed their son. His mother had recently passed away, and the house had become his responsibility. The house was paid off but, as mentioned, not in the most desirable condition. The overall structure of the home was solid, but the overpowering stench set everyone on their heels.

It took only one meeting to get this property under contract with multiple options. The seller had no interest in owning the home and didn't have the financial resources to do any maintenance or fix anything before putting it on the market. I asked him if it made sense for me simply to take over the responsibility of the home and begin managing it so that he no longer had any interest in it and didn't have to worry about it anymore. This question was code for *I will take the house from you if you want to give it to me.* You know what happened next? He agreed! I actually got the house for free by simply offering to take over all responsibilities for it. His real problem was the pain the house held for him, and his frustration at having his life interrupted to maintain the property since it was sitting vacant.

While we were working through the details of the contract, he mentioned funeral costs in passing, so I ended up offering to purchase the house for the cost of the funeral. It was the right thing to do. It still cost me only a couple thousand dollars, and I already knew how I could sell the property for a small down payment and receive monthly payments over time.

The difference between this house and the hoarder house was that I had zero plans to touch this house. I didn't plan on cleaning it. I didn't plan on doing any renovations, or even mowing the yard. I planned to resell it before we ever closed on it. I knew some people in the area who were looking for houses selling at a discount who either wanted to move in and make it their own or use it as a flip property. I chose to turn the property over quickly, selling it for a down payment and monthly payments. This time the note was paid off very quickly, so I ended up earning roughly $10,000 on a house that I virtually received for free.

Many people might ask why I didn't choose to clean up the house and sell it at the highest market price I could get. The reason that I didn't was because the market price of this house was in the $25,000 range. I would have had to put about $10,000 into it, which would have left me a spread of only around $10,000. I was able to earn this same profit without doing any work, and I was able to sell it before I closed on it with the original seller. So, I had zero work, zero responsibility, and earned the exact same amount on the deal.

The "Ranking Your Exit Strategies" in the step-by-step guide that follows explains the exact process I used.

---

**GREAT QUESTION: AM I READY TO COMMIT TO A LIFE OF DELAYED GRATIFICATION AND LONG-TERM INVESTING?**

---

## STEP ONE
# Organizing Note/Title Company

When completing any real estate transaction, you need to have a reliable title company or attorney on the backend of your deal to complete the paperwork and file the transaction so that all of your deals are recorded and legal. Having a reliable title company or attorney to keep your paperwork organized is absolutely vital.

The closing costs and fees you have to pay a professional for closings are well worth it. Hiring a professional to handle things can be the difference between losing hundreds of thousands of dollars or making hundreds of thousands on a single deal due to the clean title work you can expect. I have had multiple situations in which sellers swore that there were no liens or loans against the property, only to discover during the title search that the house was underwater with liens ranging from federal taxes to child support to bank lending. A thorough, professional title search will save you more times than you can count as you build your business. Don't even think about skipping it to save a few dollars and speed up the process.

The section on title company and attorney closings in the first book of my "I've Got Nothing For You" series contained an in-depth discussion of what to key in on when hiring one of these professionals because not all title companies or attorneys are well-versed and knowledgeable regarding real estate investments. Some may have never completed a wholesale deal, and their inexperience could result in failed paperwork. Luckily, almost all title companies are able to handle deals involving selling properties on terms using promissory notes and purchasing rental properties creatively. It is the title company's job to be a $3^{rd}$ party in the transaction and communicate clearly with both the buyer and seller. Title companies also have the ability to perform title searches and ensure that a title is clear so that when you want to place a lien on a property to secure a promissory note, having a good relationship with a title company will provide you with a team who can do so.

I highly recommend that you establish a relationship with a company before you even have any deals in the pipeline. Meet with them a few times so that they understand where you are and where you want to be as well as the requirements you will have for your deals. This open line of communication will be vital on down the road when hiccups inevitably occur, and you have to provide solutions quickly.

Understanding your title company and having a relationship with the employees of the company will also help you close more deals. Having a quality team on the backend of your deals will give you the confidence to share their contact information with your sellers and buyers. This will give the people working with you some assurance and allow them to feel comfortable doing business with you. You will be amazed how much it helps to be able to contact a buyer or seller and give him or her a direct line to a contact at the company instead of telling them, "The paperwork is at the title company." These are the small details that, when refined, will help your business continue to grow smoothly.

## GREAT QUESTION: DO I HAVE A RELIABLE TITLE COMPANY OR CLOSING ATTORNEY TO HANDLE MY PAPERWORK?

## STEP ONE
# Explaining Your Goals and Path

During your first few conversations with the title company, you should talk about your targets and plans for achieving those goals. When I am working with a company, I always make sure to establish a plan with them so that they know what to expect from me, and I can learn what they need from me to best do their work. When I first began investing, I found I created delays at times because I failed to supply the title company with all of the information that they needed to move forward with the transaction. This stuck them with the responsibility of hunting the information down, which made the process longer--and more expensive in some cases.

For example, I didn't realize that my title company preferred to have property and condition disclosures submitted with the purchase agreement. I was using a generic purchase agreement that I had found online, and it was missing key elements that the title company needed to close the deal. As a result, the title company had to contact the seller, the buyer, or me multiple times for each transaction to collect more information—information that I could have collected when I initially signed the paperwork. After learning about this, I discovered they had a contract they preferred using because it included every detail that they required. Switching to their preferred contract resulted in smoother transactions and quicker closings.

Avoid this issue by contacting multiple title companies and attorneys to learn what they need from you to best do their job. When you discover what they need, you will understand how you might provide the requisite documentation at the outset, avoiding preventable delayed closings. Taking this action first will also ensure that you will be able to outsource this step to a member of your team at some point. You will know who the contacts are and what information everyone needs so you can provide it when you are training a team member to handle this step for you. Remember the training focus is on cashflow and building freedom, not owning a well-organized job. Always be looking ahead.

After talking to multiple title companies and attorneys, you will find a company that fits your needs best. You will find a company willing to put the time-effort in you before you even have any business for them, which is important. You don't necessarily want the biggest or most popular company working for you; you want the one most focused on taking care of you and your customers. You will be able to identify this via your early conversations and relationship building efforts.

**GREAT QUESTION: AM I EXCITED TO BE WORKING WITH WHO I CHOSE TO DO MY TITLE WORK? WHY OR WHY NOT?**

## STEP ONE
# Understanding the Process

One of the early conversations with your title company and closing attorney should be focused on the title company process. More times than not, you will be pleasantly surprised at how simple it is to create a promissory note or file a lien on a property to protect yourself and your investing partners.

When we are uncertain about how a process works, we will naturally create confusion in our business and our closings. Many people think that creating a promissory note or selling a property in any creative fashion other than a cash transaction requires a different set of contracts and/or confusing paperwork when, in reality, the paperwork is the same as it is for any other transaction. You use a basic purchase agreement and simply explain the specific details of the sale to the title company.

For example, assume I want to sell a property that I own on terms, and I want to create a promissory note that specifies I will receive monthly payments versus a single lump sum. I will complete the purchase agreement with my potential buyer in the exact same fashion as I would if he or she were buying it for cash. I would then note the specifics of the transaction on the side of the contract or on a separate sheet of paper. I would indicate the terms of the sale in detail, including the agreed-upon terms of the promissory note. I provide the amount of the down payment required, the monthly payments, interest rate, length of the loan in months, total interest paid over the term of the loan, and all the contact information for both parties. At this point, both the seller (me, in this case) and the buyer sign the document. The title company now has the information it needs to create the promissory note and secure a lien against the property in my name upon closing so that I am protected against any default.

It never needs to be any more complicated than the above example. You should always refer back to your trusted title company and attorney anytime there are questions about a closing or other legal issue. We pay for these resources, and they are what keep us moving forward. The title company will always be able to tell you what is needed and many times can provide it to you so that you don't need to spend much, if any, time at all focusing on solving a problem that arises.

Understanding the details involved in the full process will result in more smooth and profitable transactions. Have you ever wondered what the title company does during those few weeks between receiving a purchase agreement and closing? Guess what? Others have, too, and the remainder of this section is devoted to explaining what to expect during a closing process and what feelings are typical during the period in which you are awaiting a closing.

Taking the time initially to set expectations and provide a timeframe for the closing process with your sellers and buyers is monumental in ensuring smooth transactions. This will eliminate the unknown, as well as the stress and anxiety of worrying if the closing will occur. Remember, you are the professional in this situation, and many times the people with whom you are working are either in stressful situations or making the largest purchase of their life. This isn't the time for poor communication. When people are stressed out and anxious, they sometimes create problems that aren't real, take up your time, and take time from your title company. This can all be avoided with a smooth intake system at the outset of the deal.

We have designed documentation and educational materials that we provide to the seller or buyer of any deal so that they can see where they are in the process and understand that the emotions and expectations they may be experiencing are common. This has been pivotal in negotiating deals that run smoothly and in unison as opposed to hectic transactions that caused constant unwanted stress.

The processes and timelines can differ company to company, but the principles discussed below will give you the foundation needed to understand the general progression and what to expect from it.

**Process and Timeline of Typical Transaction:**

**Action 1: Title company receives signed purchase agreement**

**Title Company:**

Once the paperwork is received, the title company will begin processing it and create a file on the transaction. Long story short, this is the point at which the company gets organized to run the paperwork through to the closing, checking title marketability and working on any necessary payoffs. The title company will gather any information needed that was omitted in the purchase agreement.

**Buyer and Seller:**

At this point the buyer and the seller are excited. They have come to a mutual agreement that satisfies both parties. Everyone is happy because everyone has received what they wanted. This typically lasts for only a couple of days.

**Action 2: Title Company performs title search**

**Title Company:**

After all required information is gathered and a file has been created, the title company begins the process of the title search. The title company is focused on ensuring that the property is clear of any liens and mortgages from previous transactions so that the title is clean and can be transferred without anyone else claiming an interest in the property. The title company is also making sure all previous paperwork and transfers match so that there is no cloud (any claim) on the title that could cause a delay in the closing or legal transfer.

**Buyer and Seller:**

During the title search process, the buyer and seller excitement has waned, and both parties are awaiting further instruction. The seller, if unaware of past issues, may be feeling impatient and hoping for good news if they know how a title search works. The buyer, at this point, may be feeling some anxiety because he or she wants the property, but there is really more stress on the seller. If the title comes back with issues (which happens more often than you may think), it is important for you to let both parties know that these issues happen and can be resolved very quickly in most cases. At this stage emotions are commonly pretty neutral with the hope of everything going well.

## Action 3: Title Commitment and Organization

**Title Company:**

The title company or closing attorney has now gathered information and run a chain of title to check for flaws and is now ready to move forward with the transaction. This is when you learn if there are title issues that need cleared or if the title is clean. Either way, the responsibility typically falls on the title company. If you can assist them in contacting anyone they need to get in touch with, it can be beneficial, but for the most part, you are hands-off during this process. When the title is clear, the title company prepares for closing and begins scheduling for it.

**Buyer and Seller:**

Anxiety and stress have peaked at this point for both parties. Unless the title company has stayed in constant contact with updates, a seller or buyer may feel the stress associated with uncertainty, but luckily, no contact usually means things are going smoothly. I like to tell this to the people with whom I'm working so that they don't keep bugging the title company unnecessarily. This only delays the process and adds to their stress.

The seller, at this point, is committed to moving or selling over the next couple of days or weeks and is excited about having his problem resolved. He worries that something might happen, leaving him to continue to shoulder the problem longer. Problems can range from financial difficulties to problematic properties.

The buyer, at this point, is feeling stress for a few different reasons. A retail buyer using a traditional mortgage to purchase the property has been going through the loan process, so he or she is attempting to pack, organize, and gather information for the lender, while taking care of normal daily responsibilities on top of it. This can be overwhelming, to say the least. A buyer who is either paying cash for the property or using seller financing is hoping for a smooth transaction so he or she can begin moving on their project ASAP. These buyers may also hope that they will not be forced to find another property, especially if facing a time crunch.

**Action 4: Closing**

**Title Company:**

Both the buyer and seller are contacted to schedule a closing date and time for the signing of the documents. The title company provides all appropriate paperwork and documentation. After each party signs and funds are collected from the buyer, the title company processes the paperwork and payment. After all is cleared, the title company files the transaction with the county to legalize the transfer. Once filed, the deal is done. The title company receives the closing costs accrued by both buyer and seller. Depending on the company or attorney, the costs may vary party to party.

**Buyer and Seller:**

Both buyer and seller are feeling relief. The worries of any possible issues, appraisals, loan agreements and approvals, inspections, title problems, and reneges are now a thing of the past. The seller is getting exactly what he needed, and the buyer is getting the property he wanted. Each party signs the paperwork at the title company, and the funds are passed from the buyer to the title company. After filing, the keys are passed to the buyer by the title company. Each party gets to move on with their life.

You can use the above descriptions to educate anyone with whom you are working to help your transactions proceed more smoothly and quickly. You may underestimate the importance of this now, but when you have a few deals that become problematic and realize that you might have been able to prevent it by being proactive, you will understand the importance of setting expectations and, more importantly, having all parties understand what they should be doing and feeling at any given time during the process.

---

**GREAT QUESTION: HOW DO I SET BETTER EXPECTATIONS IN MY BUSINESS AND IN MY PERSONAL LIFE?**

---

## STEP TWO
# Locating Property at Discount by Locating Larger Problems to Solve

In order to create options with multiple profitable exit strategies, we need to find larger and larger problems to solve for people. There are literally hundreds of ways to find possible sellers who have some sort of need or motivation to sell a property. What if we don't want to find just anyone, though? What if we want to find only the most motivated people, those with the largest problems and who may possibly need to move quickly as well? How can we pinpoint our marketing to increase our conversions and decrease our cost per sale? The answer to these questions lies in our focus and approach.

The general consensus is that the more people you touch with a marketing piece the better, but truth be told, touching the BEST people with your marketing is much more important. Using free marketing tactics to touch as many people as possible can be beneficial because it can help create a reputation for yourself and build a consistent image. However, when we are paying actual dollars for our marketing, we want it to be laser-focused on specific criteria that allow us to locate those with the largest and most compelling problems that we can solve and close on. If you need suggestions and some marketing training, make sure to check out the first book in this series if you haven't already (*If You Can't Wholesale After This.. I've Got Nothing For You*). It has specific sections on how to market to sellers, including a step-by-step guide.

Rather than marketing and networking with a "shotgun" approach wherein you are simply blasting out your information to anyone who will look at it and many who won't, you need to zero in on only the most motivated sellers who have serious pain points. When you do so, you'll be solving larger problems for people, such as rescuing people from bad inheritances, bankruptcy, foreclosure, and even tax and IRS liens.

I have a method of pairing multiple pain points or larger pain points together that I call "stacking." This means I am touching on multiple pain points at once. This puts a certain pressure on a seller, which makes him more amenable to let you solve his problem for him. Remember, none of this is possible if the seller isn't reasonable and, to some extent, open to receiving help. When we "stack" pain points, we tend to get better results.

Stacking multiple pain points enables us to create specific solutions and motivators. When someone has inherited a house that he or she doesn't want, that's certainly a pain point, but there is no real timetable for a solution. If someone has a house that he or she inherits but doesn't want, that person can sit on that property until the end of time if he or she wants. But what if there was a pending tax foreclosure on this property that you could help remedy? Now that person has a property that he or she neither loves nor wants, and a serious timetable for action, due to a pending tax foreclosure that will affect his/her credit or financial strength. In this situation your ability to help is a no-brainer.

When we focus on stacking larger problems like the ones in this example, we begin solving problems so large that the numbers no longer matter to the seller. When the numbers no longer matter, we have the ability to negotiate great buys and purchase property at discounts, which allows us to implement multiple strategies and exit plans. You make your money on the "buy" in this game. When you buy property at a great price, it's tough not to win! This is why buying during down markets and recessions is a smart move more times than not. We are looking to do the opposite of the general public.

You can find these larger problems that are crying for solutions in a multitude of ways, but one of the single greatest tools you can use is your own voice.

You need to be telling absolutely everyone what you do and what solutions you can provide for people. You may start out slow, but the longer and more consistently you practice this simple marketing tool the more opportunities you will attract as people get to know you. With time, you'll find more and more people who have problems.

You need to have an organized and focused approach with your direct marketing  This will allow you to scale and maintain consistent lead generation. Again, don't use a shotgun approach that is focused on anyone and everyone. Instead, focus on specific pain points and touch these potential sellers by mentioning the specific pain point directly in the marketing piece.

For example, when using direct marketing, don't mail your ads to an entire zip code, street, or town just because the house is in the area that you like. Instead, narrow down these leads and pair symptoms of the problems you solve with the marketing piece. If you want to solve inheritance issues, you need to locate the property and its new owner by researching the probate records at the courthouse and target the new owner with a direct mail ad that asks, "Have an unwanted inherited property?"

If you want to focus on saving people from foreclosure, you need to create a list of properties in areas within which you want to own property and match them with pre-foreclosure files at your county courthouse. That way you are assured that you have an extremely motivated seller with a short timeline and a property that you know you would be proud to own—a seller with whom you can work to create more motivation and opportunity. This practice of stacking multiple motivations will help improve your conversion rate and reduce your marketing expenses.

Each market and courthouse is slightly different, so you want to ensure you are staying within the laws and regulations of each state and local government, but in general, the principle is simple: match real problems with properties you actually want in order to improve your conversion rate. If it is illegal to focus on pre-foreclosure leads in your area, you can still focus on other pain points to help people. Do your due diligence and research upfront so that your marketing becomes laser-focused.

You can buy lead lists from different online sources as well. This is perfectly fine, but you will need to refine these lists with extreme precision. It's a good idea to review the list you purchase and consider what sellers may be most motivated or which properties you are interested in most so that you are, once again, hitting the people with the best motivations as well as property that truly interests you. There are endless online resources for creating seller-lead lists. A couple of my favorites are listsource.com and rebogateway. Each of these resources allows you to customize and filter the leads using different criteria, enabling you to match pain point symptoms to possible properties in areas you want.

I will provide more pain point examples and methods to locate sellers with these problems, but first let's examine pairing pain points with properties. If you need more specific training on how to market, please revisit the first book in this series: *If You Can't Wholesale After This.. I've Got Nothing For You*. You will find examples of actual letters and the wording therein in the section titled "Step 3: Marketing to Problems" on pages 44-58.

---

**GREAT QUESTION: AM I LOOKING TO SOLVE MULTIPLE PROBLEMS AT ONCE, OR AM I ATTEMPTING TO FORCE A SINGLE SOLUTION ON A SINGLE PROBLEM THAT MAY BE LESS SEVERE THAN I ONCE THOUGHT?**

---

## STEP TWO
# What to Look for

When we locate problems to solve and manage to stack a few pain points together, thus creating the possibility of a great buy for ourselves, we need to remember that the property is still the most important investment at the end of the day. We don't want to pair problems with property that isn't worth the work or the headache that dealing with it may cause. We want to stack problems to solve in areas with properties that we want to purchase and will be proud to have in our portfolio. These properties will differ from person to person, but every investor needs to understand the concept of building value. Understanding true building value is what will allow for win-win situations and great buys that flourish over time.

Generally speaking, if we pair a handful of problems with a property that has serious foundation issues in a neighborhood that we don't love or in which we don't have much of a network, we aren't guaranteeing ourselves a win. Now, if we pair these stacked problems with a property in an area we are specifically targeting to add to or create our portfolio and we manage to create a great buy on a property that has good building value, we are going to win and increase our wealth. So, what is good building value? Let's cover that now.

Many people refer to building value as "good bones," or a multitude of other terms. When evaluating property, you need to understand the factors that can cause excess costs and issues. When I personally am considering building value, I want a solid roof, newer windows, updated mechanicals, and a solid foundation. This immediately eliminates early issues that can blow up a budget (right, spreadsheet warriors?) and create higher-than-normal maintenance and holding costs. When you fail to think about building value, you will find yourself spending more and more money as time passes, due to higher-than-normal insurance costs, maintenance costs, utilities, and labor costs, and you'll be plagued with constant calls and complaints from your tenants. So, is this really a win in the long term, even if you managed to purchase it below market price? Not really! I want property that someone else has already updated at some point, if need be, so that our long-term asset is strong. Remember, we are thinking long term now! We are no longer thinking short-term cash or flips.

With multiple pain points stacked and paired with a property that has a great foundation, newer windows, updated mechanicals, and a roof that is going to last, you create a buy that allows multiple different strategies to exist and live alongside each other. You are buying larger-than-normal equity, as well as the ability to cashflow a property month-to-month. If you borrowed the money for the purchase, your debt service is more manageable. You also have the ability to sell to a partner or end buyer on terms, and you may even do a combination of these over time. This also allows for yet more creative options down the road. Once the property is up and running, you can borrow against it since it is in good working condition and you bought it below market rate. This, in turn, will enable you to use the same money more than once to buy more properties when the time comes. Pairing problem solving with great building value is the single quickest way to build your wealth in real estate. Normally, properties of this type come at a premium, so your ability to find these and buy below market rate will open your business up for growth.

Notice that I didn't mention cosmetics and lighter maintenance and rehab issues. This is because cosmetic issues can be quick and affordable fixes to make the property one that fits your criteria. Having a new bathroom installed for a couple thousand dollars is not only a tax write-off, but can last a customer of yours for many years. Every year your customer stays put, you build wealth.

Properties that are really ugly but have great building value have great profit potential because you will have the vision and long-term mindset to look beyond the ugly and focus on the strong points of the future asset. Paint costs less than foundation issues over 10 years. The nice thing is that when the house is ugly, the typical buyer will stay away from it because he or she will fail to see its potential. This creates even more opportunity for you; you can capitalize on it in your negotiations. I once bought a house with a new roof, new windows, a four-seasons sun room, new furnace and water tank, brand-new air conditioning unit, new siding, and great foundation for $50,000 when the house was worth $100,000 because every wall in the house was bright yellow, pink, and blue, with scrapes and peeling all over. It was ugly! The flooring needed sanded and stained. The appliances needed replaced, and the countertop needed redone. This few-thousand-dollar fix created over $40,000 in equity for me instantly.

Let me tell you how I negotiated the purchase of this house. I got the lead from someone who had done work for my company previously and was looking for more remodeling work. A couple had seen his social media posts and contacted him. While he was refinishing a bathroom for them, he overheard them talking about the woman's father and how they needed to sell his house as soon as possible because he was going into a nursing home. Long story short, the rehabber put them in contact with me, and I asked them what they needed. They explained that other prospective buyers had passed on the house because of the condition and that $50,000 was all they needed. We signed that day. We closed a couple weeks later, and I bought $40,000-plus in equity. Not a bad bump in net worth, which I got because I understood building value and had some experience with what cosmetic repairs cost and look like. This property now produces over $1,100 a month in cashflow, and I can borrow against it or sell it at any time. Repeating this process over and over with extreme focus is what creates wealth.

Now let's talk about pairing the pain points in this property while taking building value into consideration. I already mentioned all the new updates and benefits of this property's building value. It also happened to be in an area that I love! I would own the entire zip code in which this property is located if I could. The pain points of the seller were perfect for creating a smooth deal as well. Her father was headed to a nursing home; they didn't have a great relationship; she had neither the resources nor the desire to keep the house; and her husband had no interest in fixing it. All of these pain points created motivation and a timeline. The pending nursing home was the timeline creator, while the poor relationship and lack of desire for the house created the motivation for selling at a price point that made sense and didn't have to be top market dollar. This is WIN-WIN! The house has been a homerun ever since. Always stack motivations and pair them with a property with real building value to maximize reward and limit risk.

Now let me tell you exactly what I look for in a property beyond just building value. I am always looking for potential and past performance, but I look at specific building types as well. This discussion will be specific to single family residences, but it can also be translated into multifamily dwellings in certain scenarios.

You will commonly find that investors who struggle will buy anything that makes sense, while investors who flourish buy specific criteria or building types. The reason for this is that not all building types and houses have the same risks and rewards.

My team and I look specifically for single-floor properties or properties with no plumbing on the second floor. The reason for this, which I learned the hard way, was that plumbing on the second floor becomes problematic and exponentially more expensive to service because when there is an issue, the first floor needs repair as well. Water damage is a serious problem in properties. Having properties with only a single floor eliminates this problem, and they are also less expensive to maintain, which directly correlates with our long-term profitability goal. Multiple stories typically means more windows and flooring. My mentor taught me long ago that your two biggest expenses in holding property are vacancies and flooring. When you own a multiple-story home or building, you will have more flooring expense and more utility and holding costs when a vacancy occurs. Over time these small issues add up to big-time dollars.

When you combine specific building types with specific building values, you will own a very specific type of real estate portfolio that will allow you to grow and know what to expect as you gain more experience. Single-story homes typically have fewer windows and a smaller footprint as well, which can translate to lower taxes, utility bills, holding costs, maintenance, and repair. If there is a single family, one-story home with three bedrooms that will rent for $1,000 a month and there is a three-story, three-bedroom home that will rent for $1,000 a month, the single-story home will be more profitable every time, barring any outstanding occurrence or issue. When you apply this to your goal of long-term growth and ask yourself *What if I had 50 more of these; what would my life look like?* you will begin to see that limiting potential problems becomes extremely important. The 50- house portfolio of ranch-style (single-story) homes will outperform the 50-house portfolio of multiple-story homes.

How else can we refine our portfolio so that it generates repeatable and free flowing cashflow? What about roof type? Do we want to focus on single family homes with pitched roofs, or do we want to focus on multifamily style buildings with more problematic flat roofs? Do we understand the costs associated with changing in the future? Do we understand tiles and material types? Do we only want homes with metal roofing? What about basements? Do we like houses with basements, or do we want to focus on slab-style housing? Are we going to buy only brick homes? Are we okay with vinyl siding? Do we want to invest in mobile homes or pre-manufactured homes? These are all things you can decide to focus on—or not--to continue to refine your portfolio to what works best for you and your team.

The single greatest way to protect yourself in real estate investment is always to buy building value and understand your portfolio plan. If you buy a property with building value, your chances for future profits are much greater than if you focus only on the sale or number at hand.

## GREAT QUESTION: DO I UNDERSTAND BUILDING VALUE?

## STEP TWO
# Understanding Problem-Solving

So, what pain points can we focus on? There are literally hundreds of reasons people need to sell a house. I covered these in the first book in this series. Some of my favorite pain points, along with their stacking category/quality, are provided below:

1. **Pre-foreclosure** – financial pain point as well as timeline creator due to pending foreclosure

2. **Probate** – severe illness followed by death causes emotional and financial stress. Can also be timeline creator

3. **Tax foreclosure** – stress from IRS, extreme need for capital, and timeline creator

4. **Inheritance** – stress caused by added responsibility along with possible financial stress

5. **Bankruptcy** – financial stress and possible timeline creator if bankruptcy can be avoided

6. **Code violations** – financial stress

7. **Tired landlord** – Possible financial stress, but responsibility associated with ownership is greater stressor

8. **Maintenance issues** – Stress of responsibility and financial stress

9. **Divorce** – emotional stress, financial stress, timeline creator

10. **Old age** – liquidating property is a more minor stress on the timeline if it doesn't have to be done

These are only a handful of problems that we have the ability to solve, but if you noticed, these problems are all much more severe than the traditional motivations implied by statements like, "I want to move," or "I'm open to selling if…." These are all great problems to stack with one another as well. You may get a great deal from a tired landlord who is fed up with tenants and the responsibility of ownership, but how much more motivated is that same landlord if he happens to have maintenance issues and faces an impending divorce? That hits all problem types! These things really happen, too. We just have to open ourselves and our marketing up to it.

Problem-solving is not an easy topic to teach or learn. I'm going to be completely honest and upfront with you. This will take time, practice, and frustration, peppered with a lot of mistakes in the process. Eventually, you will become extremely skilled in listening for specific key words and matching them with specific solutions that work for both parties. I will teach you the types of conversations on which you should focus your attention.

We want to do a lot of listening, and I have an entire section dedicated to questions and how to pair specific solutions to specific problems, but in this section, I want to focus on the proper mindset for problem solving. We need to have the ability to reach outside ourselves and put ourselves in the shoes of the potential seller and see and feel what would truly solve the problem at hand. Many times, the seller will not come out and state the real problem right off the bat. There may be times that they deny any money problems and indicate that they are only tired of the responsibility, but you may see evidence to indicate that money is the real problem at hand. Let's talk about what you can look for in this situation and how you can begin breaking down the problem-solving process.

## Diagnosis – Getting to the root of the pain

Much like a doctor, therapist, mechanic, or inventor, you won't have the ability to solve the problem at hand without first diagnosing it. Your doctor can't treat you before he or she understands what is ailing you, right? This applies to creating solutions in real estate, as well.

On an even broader level, breaking down problems and beginning with diagnosis will solve other issues in your life, too. Gaining clarity by breaking down the problems at hand step-by-step will allow you to take better and quicker actions and will help provide a clearer path to whatever solution or result you desire.

Diagnosing the problem at hand begins with asking great questions and focusing on listening to the answers. You cannot diagnose someone else's problem by talking yourself. Again, think about when you go to the doctor or to an auto mechanic. They tend to ask you a number of questions and listen to your (or your car's) symptoms. You need to do the same thing. Listen for the symptoms of the pain that a piece of property is causing so that you can provide the correct solution for it.

**Designing Solutions – Brainstorming and sharing possible solutions to the problem at hand**

After gathering enough information to diagnose a possible problem to solve, we want to provide possible solutions to the seller. It is entirely possible that multiple solutions can remedy a singular pain, but providing more than one option that will work for you will allow the seller to choose the one that works best for him or her as well. This will also provide even more information to what the true pain may be. Ask yourself why the seller chose or declined certain solutions to his or her problem, and you may find that your diagnosis needs to be re-evaluated.

**Re-evaluate Diagnosis and Solution Pairing – Working to fit a better solution to a problem different from the one originally diagnosed**

When providing multiple solutions to the problem at hand, we want to think about and reconsider other possible solutions. Is the solution that the seller chose or declined the best possible answer to the problem at hand?

We want to work closely with the seller to design the best possible solution to relieve his or her pain and create a worthwhile investment for ourselves that will pay us for years to come, with minimal risk.

There is often new information provided after the diagnosis stage. When a seller has accepted or declined multiple offers, it provides valuable data that you can use before finalizing the deal. For example, a seller may have responded negatively to solutions wherein his or her responsibility in a property is relieved, but he/she isn't walking away with a bunch of cash after closing. This can be a sign that you missed a financial pain point that exists in addition to the pain point of the responsibilities for maintenance or other issues that come with property ownership. Be open-minded and totally neutral in this information-gathering stage. If you get emotional in any way, the seller will follow suit, and any deal will be in jeopardy.

In re-evaluating an offer, you will recognize that people are ashamed of their problems, so it may take a few tries before getting to the real pain to solve. Be aware of this before ever making your first offer and understand this is a journey and a process. It is rare that the first offer you make is immediately accepted.

**Apply Solution and Perform Accordingly – Solution is accepted, and you perform to the best of your ability**

At this point the seller has chosen from among multiple problem-solving options, and you move towards the closing table. It is good to follow up with the seller and reassure him or her as the process unfolds. You should also follow up with your process and review how everything unfolded. Consider all the data that you now have at your fingertips. What was the true problem? What questions were asked? How many solutions were provided? How long did it take to unveil the true pain and provide a solution to it? Answering all of these questions and tracking your data over time will allow you to diagnose problems better in the future and provide superior solutions quicker. You will be refining your process and business at this point!

---

**GREAT QUESTION: AM I FOCUSED ON LISTENING FOR THE TRUE PAIN IN SOMEONE'S VOICE AND STORY SO THAT I CAN PROVIDE THE BEST POSSIBLE SOLUTION TO THEM?**

---

# STEP TWO
# WHAT TO SAY AND WHAT QUESTIONS TO ASK

It is in the quality of questions that we ask that we will find the pain of our sellers, if any true pain exists. If no true pain exists, the questions will enable you to decide more quickly whether or not you will be doing a deal with the seller. The time it will take you will get shorter and shorter as you improve as an information gatherer and investor. Let's cover some great questions that my partners and I use every day in order to gather more information so that we can better help.

**Questions:**

1. Why do you want to sell?
2. What is it like owning this property?
3. How did you acquire this property?
4. How long have you been the owner?
5. What is the best way I can serve you?
6. Have you considered different options?
7. Why is now the time to sell?
8. Have you ever tried to sell previously?

9. What other offers have you considered?
10. What is the most important thing to get out of this sale?
11. If you owned this house for another handful of years, what would your life look like?
12. Does this house cause some sort of pain?
13. Do you hold any love for or connection with this house?
14. Are there any issues with the property you can't handle?
15. Would you like to keep this house if you could?
16. Why not keep the house?
17. Have you considered selling in the past?
18. How can I best relieve your pain in this house?
19. Does it make sense to you for me simply to take over the responsibilities of this house?
20. Have you ever had issues with the neighborhood?
21. Do you like the neighborhood?
22. Do you like the neighbors?
23. If you kept the house, what would you do with it?
24. Will selling this house save you from something such as bankruptcy or another foreclosure?
25. What do you think this house is worth?

The above questions will serve to direct your diagnosis and information-gathering process. You obviously won't have to ask each and every question each time, but the list provides a great example of the types of questions you should be asking to gauge whether the seller has a real pain or is just looking for top dollar.

Typically, when a seller is only looking for top dollar, recommending that the seller put it on the market is the best solution because that is how he or she will get the most for the property. We don't need to stress over solving every problem for every person. Sellers need to be open to solutions as well, and we want to be solving problems for people, not adopting their problems. There is a big difference between those two things! Remember, we always make our money on the "buy," so we must pair solutions that work for us with problems that the seller presents to us.

While the seller is answering the above questions, be very focused on listening, and you can identify where the seller shows the most passion and emotion. This will typically help pinpoint the true pain in the property. If a seller can consistently slide over responsibility issues but begins to become emotional when talking about money or financial issues, you will typically find that money is the true pain at hand. Keep an eye out for body language and an ear out for tone of voice when listening to the answers the seller provides. Again, you will get better at this with practice.

Once the seller begins talking, stay quiet and keep body motion to a minimum. You don't want to sway anyone one way or another. You just want to focus on being there for the seller, and to do that you must be neutral and understanding.

As an example, have you ever noticed how nodding your head at certain points in a conversation tends to lead the conversation more in that direction? This is what we don't necessarily want. We want our sellers to be open and talking about their true pain. If we start nodding at everything they say, they will get confused, and you will have no real direction in your conversation anymore. Just let them know you are listening if they pause, and they will open up to you.

---

**GREAT QUESTION: AM I INFLUENCING THESE CONVERSATIONS WITH SELLERS MORE THAN I REALIZE, MAKING IT TAKE LONGER TO GET TO A REAL PAIN POINT?**

---

## STEP TWO
# Understanding Sellers Don't Want Money

---

Sellers don't necessarily want money; they want the problem solved. Keeping this in mind will open you up to so many more brainstorming ideas and solutions that will make a deal work. More often than not, when people get into real estate, they think money solves all problems. This isn't the case. In the previous sections we learned that we need to be asking great questions and diagnosing a problem in order to provide multiple solutions and create a great investment. Understand that people don't necessarily want money--because money is just a tool--they want what they believe the money will give them. It's up to you to figure out what that is, using your problem-solving process.

When looking for problems to solve, we want to focus on problems for which we can provide creative solutions. When someone says they need $50,000 for the house, what he or she means is, "I'm in pain due to a back-tax lien or other financial issue that I need $50,000 to remedy." It can be any type of financial pain, but the key is figuring out what the pain actually is. It can be uncomfortable, but ask the seller how the $50,000 will help. You will be shocked at how often the problem doesn't require a lump sum solution. Maybe it is a $50,000 debt obligation that requires monthly payments of $300.

When we hear problems like the one above, we see immediate opportunity. "What if I handled that debt for you?" The seller agrees that sounds great, and in handling the debt, you may find you can negotiate that debt down on their behalf. Then you have the ability to own a property for much less than the original asking price of $50,000. Maybe you can negotiate that debt down to a required monthly payment of only $150 per month, and you plan on renting the property for $1,000 per month. That sounds like a solid investment! This type of creative thinking is what will allow you to grow your portfolio without having to take any dollars out of your own pocket.

Another great example of this is when people are burdened with medical bills. Medical bills are typically the easiest to negotiate down due to such a high rate of delinquency on them. When we have sellers with medical-bill stress, we can provide multiple different solutions that will eliminate their bills, while we receive a great property in return.

Remember, in the pain of the seller there is a need. The need isn't always money. They want what they think the money will provide them. Ask them how you can provide that "something" instead, and you can make a trade!

---

**GREAT QUESTION: DO I UNDERSTAND THAT PEOPLE DON'T TRULY WANT MONEY, BUT WANT WHAT THEY THINK THE MONEY WILL BRING THEM?**

---

## STEP TWO
# How to Pair a Solution to Any Problem

Once we diagnose a problem, we have the ability to provide a solution that works for both parties. The great part about this approach is that many times we have the ability to provide solutions the seller didn't know existed, and we don't have to take any money out of our own pockets to control a new potential asset.

The most important piece to pairing a solution to a problem is understanding the problem at hand. When you understand the problem, you can dissect it and pair it with a solution that provides the most relief over time for the seller.

For example, assume someone has bad debt due to a property that is costing them monthly, hurting their cashflow, and causing them financial stress. The best solution isn't necessarily to sell the house outright for a lump sum because there is the possibility that the lump sum may not pay off the debts. Furthermore, there may be other factors to consider, including taxes and fees. Taking income and expenses into account, you may decide that the best solution is for you to buy the house from the seller on terms, giving him or her a promissory note and lien position. The terms of the note could stipulate that you will pay the seller the monthly amount that his/her debt is currently costing as long as the rental income you receive from the house is greater than that amount. This allows the seller to be freed from the monthly payments of that debt and relieves his/her financial stress. This is just one possible creative solution to the problem.

I personally like to rank and categorize solutions to specific types of problems. In understanding what problems create great solutions, I have the ability to pair solutions easily to different types of problems.

Any monthly payment problems or monthly income issues can be solved by paying sellers over time rather than paying a lump sum for the property. This immediately lowers my out-of-pocket cost, so I need fewer resources to solve the problem at hand.

When a seller has maintenance issues that he or she can't handle, I know that I can remedy it with a lump sum solution or monthly payment plan because the real pain is responsibility. If I take over the responsibility, any monetary benefit is just a bonus.

Anytime a seller needs to sell very quickly, I know that I can use a lump sum payment since he or she won't have to deal with a buyer who needs a traditional loan that can take 45 days to secure. Alternatively, I can dig deeper and learn the reason he or she needs to sell so quickly. If the reason isn't financial, I can provide solutions wherein I take over responsibility for any debt owed, and the seller can walk away.

Understand that any and all problems have a solution. Having an open mind to pairing solutions with problems instead of believing that only money solves problems will allow you to pair a solution to any problem out there. It is up to the seller to accept the help!

---

**GREAT QUESTION: DO I HAVE AN OPEN MIND TO PAIRING PROBLEMS WITH SOLUTIONS CONSISTENTLY?**

---

# STEP THREE
# WHAT CAN I PAY FOR THIS PROPERTY?

As I have already noted a couple of times, we make our money on the "buy" in this game. No matter how we buy the property--whether it be in a traditional fashion or a creative fashion--it is important to stick to the criteria and a threshold that we have established. We can't just pay any price for a property and hope that we make it back when we sell it or rent it. We need to understand monthly debt services, holding costs, fees, taxes, and miscellaneous costs. All of this information will provide us with a target price or maximum price that we can offer and still ensure ourselves a profit on the deal.

With that being said, there is no golden formula that will work for everyone or be attractive to every investor. Different markets and fluctuations mandate different expenses and purchase prices. Nevertheless, there is a single truth in real estate, regardless of your business strategy. It doesn't matter if you will be selling on terms, fixing and flipping, renting single family homes, or buying commercial buildings that will enable you to recoup your investment and make a profit. That truth is that you make your money on the "buy"!

When you purchase a property based on established criteria for less than its market value, you are maximizing your opportunity because you can profit in multiple ways. There have been times that my team and I purchased a property with the intention of fixing it and flipping it for a profit, but then discovered it was a property that we wanted to hold in our portfolio of rental properties. We would never enjoy this flexibility if we failed to stick to our criteria and making our money on the "buy." When you adhere to your set criteria and buy property at a discount, you have more flexibility and liquidity. If at any point you need to sell, you can. This is key for your long-term growth.

The mindset necessary to do this is simple, but it can be painful at times. You may feel a connection to a seller or a house and truly want to purchase it even though it doesn't make sense for an investment. The ability to say no and pass on those properties will help your business grow more than being able to say yes at any point will. I promise you that.

I previously shared the type of building and property that we like to purchase. I highly recommend that you establish specific building criteria for yourself so that you are focused only on the properties that make the most sense for you and your business. That being said, how do the numbers break down? We need to know our numbers, right? Let's cover that now.

Again, there are no golden formulas that will guarantee your success, but I can teach you the principles that will help protect you and let you know what to expect regarding your income and expenses so that you are ensuring the most profit possible per unit of investment.

**Expenses to Expect:**
1. **Debt service**
2. **Maintenance**
3. **Management**
4. **Taxes**
5. **Insurance**
6. **Repair allocation**
7. **Vacancy**

As you can see right off the bat, there is a handful of expenses that you won't be able to escape completely, but you will be able to organize and minimize these over time. When you purchase a property that you plan to hold as a cashflow generator, you need to consider these expenses. If you don't include each of these in your expense estimates, there is a very good chance that you will find yourself paying more than you are bringing in.

As mentioned in a previous section, your highest expenses will be vacancy and flooring. Flooring can fall under "repair allocation" or "maintenance;" it doesn't matter. Just be aware these will be your two largest expenses on a rental property as time marches on. Let's cover each expense in an example.

Sample property: Purchase price was $50,000. We borrowed the $50,000 for purchase, repayable at $300 per month. The property will rent for $1,200 per month.

Rental income $1,200

Debt Service - $300

Maintenance -$120

Management - $120

Taxes -$100

Insurance -$50

Repair Allocation -$100

Vacancy -$120

Utilities -Paid by tenant, but be aware of what they can be since you will be paying them when the property is vacant.

You can see how quickly our $1,200 in rental revenue resulted in a net profit of only $290 after paying expenses out of that income. With the exception of taxes, you can typically adjust these numbers slightly, but if the only way a property can make sense is by ignoring an expense that will need to be paid, you need to reconsider the investment. Perhaps you can negotiate a different purchase price or different terms for the debt owed. Everything in real estate is a negotiation at the end of the day, but this property needs to fit the criteria that you establish for your business.

Sample criteria: Property must be a ranch-style home; 20% equity, $350 per month of positive cashflow after expenses; have good building value.

If this was your criteria, the sample property provided in the example would not fit the bill. You would need to renegotiate the purchase price because the property doesn't produce enough monthly cashflow. You want $350 a month, and its estimated cashflow is only $290 a month. This is where it can be difficult to say no if you feel a connection with the seller or the property. The cashflow isn't off by much, but when you establish purchase criteria, you need to stick to your list in order to protect yourself and your business.

When considering what you can pay for a property, review the estimated income and expenses first. Then determine the payment amount that the property can support. The payment terms may indicate that you can pay a higher price than you originally thought, but my team and I enjoy having equity in the property and the option to exit the property at any time, so we don't base our purchase price solely on the terms of the loan we will be using.

Whether using a traditional loan or private lenders, you can use mortgage calculators to get an idea of what you can pay others for borrowing their capital. Again, real estate can be leveraged, and the loans are secured by real property, so money is all around you. Understanding your market and how the numbers work will also enable you to set hard stops on your offers and will allow you to negotiate better deals with sellers. This will take time, but you will get better at it over time. This is, once again, a practice.

If one of your criteria is equity, make sure that you design it so that you have some flexibility as the market moves. If you plan on flipping a property, be certain to include a minimum estimated profit in your list of criteria. There is no reason to risk $200,000 for a potential profit of $12,000. If you are flipping a property, make sure you are going to make at least $25,000 each time to protect yourself from surprise issues that occur more often than anyone would like to admit. Squatter house…(cough!)

---

**GREAT QUESTION: AM I LASER-FOCUSED ON MY PURCHASE PRICE AND STICKING TO A LIST OF CRITERIA?**

---

# STEP THREE
# Exit Strategies

When you focus on buying property at a discount, you introduce flexibility and options into your business. It is important to have options! Having flexibility creates liquidity and protects you during market downturns and potential recessions that may occur while you are in the middle of projects. If you buy a property to flip, and it will only work as a flip and never a rental, due to the purchase price and debt service, you add unnecessary risk to your business. If the market were to correct and pull back while you are in the middle of multiple projects that depend on a strong market, what will happen to your business? Your business and personal life will suffer as these no-cashflow "assets" will quickly become large liabilities. The more no-cashflow investments you have, the more risk and liability you are accepting as a business owner and provider.

Cashflow is king! Consistent, repetitive, long-term cashflow is your key to building a recession-proof foundation that allows you to capitalize on more opportunities and reach greater heights. Focus your exit strategies on paying you hundreds of times, not just once. There is no doubt that flipping a property for a lump sum can be beneficial in raising capital or capitalizing on an opportunity, but you get paid only once if you sell the property in a traditional fashion. You then need to start the process over and find another property, and this costs you more in time and money. Why not make that same $30,000 profit last 15 years instead of just one or two months?

Before covering some of the most popular deal types and exit strategies and discussing how to turn them into reliable cashflow machines, let's cover some of the risks involved with investing in non-cashflow assets and structuring deals that pay out only once.

Non-cashflow assets, once again, are investment projects that have no plan for paying out more than one lump sum. These can be fix and flip projects, restructuring projects (such as converting a commercial building into a single-family home), or the purchase of raw land with the thought of flipping it or developing it. Now, all of these strategies can be extremely profitable with the right team, process, and market. Unfortunately, no one has a crystal ball, and if any of these strategies require an upmarket, you put yourself at risk of being stuck "holding the bag." If, instead, we primarily concentrate on cashflow assets and wholesaling, we limit our risk and have a hedge against the risk involved in larger projects, such as the previously mentioned fix and flips and/or raw land development deals.

When you structure your projects and deals so that they will always benefit you for years down the road, it will undoubtedly take you a little bit longer to build a million-dollar savings account, but it will ensure that you have consistent income for the rest of your life. I don't know about you, but if I have the choice of getting a million dollars one time or $20,000 per month for life, I'm taking the $20,000. This is delayed gratification!

Investors don't typically get rich in strong markets that have been at a peak for an extended amount of time. We are contrarians. Great investors make their biggest net worth jumps during down markets because down markets provide massive opportunity. To capitalize on markets that are down, you must be liquid, flexible, and prepared to purchase when everyone else is scared to do so.

Next, let's discuss how to structure some of the most popular transaction types so that you can profit for years to come.

## GREAT QUESTION: AM I PREPARED FOR A DOWN MARKET?

# STEP THREE
# WHOLESALE

The first book in the "I've Got Nothing For You" series was dedicated strictly to wholesaling. Wholesaling can be a great way to get started in real estate with no money or experience and minimal risk. The problem with wholesaling is that people get stuck in collecting single checks for the sale of properties instead of considering how to structure their deals in such a way that they get paid hundreds of times. As we have discussed in this book, that isn't a great mindset for creating long-term wealth unless you are building a business around it that it can sustain itself without your daily interaction.

What few realize is that you can sell your wholesale contracts creatively in a way that will allow you to be paid many times over. This exit strategy is similar to the promissory notes strategy we discussed earlier. If you recall, we discussed creating a promissory note and selling your interest in a property on terms, with a lien position on the property, instead of selling it for one lump sum. Similarly, we want to focus on creating win-win deals with investors looking for property, allowing them to pay us over time. This ensures consistent income that we can continue to build on with the passage of time. The first couple $100 checks may not be life-changing, but when you can repeat the process 10 times in the first few months of transitioning to long-term cashflow, you will realize the benefits.

Don't forget: when you own debt, you own an asset that you can sell for a lump sum at any time, so you are creating an investment that has some liquidity and flexibility as well. This is a great way to create income that allows you to capitalize on more opportunity in the future with minimum risk.

The process for wholesaling on terms is quick and easy. Simply negotiate your original purchase agreement with your seller and then create an assignment contract stipulating the terms of the sale. If you are accepting any money down, you can note it at this time, and the seller and the buyer will both sign off on the agreed-upon terms and profits. This ensures that everyone is aware of the process at hand and how the transaction is being completed. Never forget that we want to be acting with 100% transparency and disclosing everything. It's okay to be making money! You are creating value in the marketplace and solving problems for people.

When creating the assignment sheet with the terms of the sale, be certain to have all contact information for the buyer listed, along with the term of the loan, the interest rate, the total interest paid over the entire term of the loan, and the amount of the monthly payments. This enables the title company or closing attorney to draw up a promissory note that you and the buyer will sign. Upon closing, your lien position on the property will be recorded so that you are protected. After this is complete, you will receive the monthly payments you have been promised, and you will have zero responsibility or ownership in the property unless the buyer fails to pay. If the buyer fails to pay at any point, you can begin the foreclosure process and take ownership in the property, which enables you to recoup any missed payments owed. If this were ever to happen, realize that you have received payments for an amount of time and now own a property free and clear.

---

**GREAT QUESTION: DO I WANT PAID TO RECEIVE ONE $5,000 PAYMENT OR $8,500 OVER FOUR YEARS, WITH INTEREST INCLUDED?**

---

# STEP THREE
# WHOLETALE

The art of the wholetale is very similar to a wholesale transaction, but nets a much larger profit in almost all situations. Wholetale has been defined in the past in multiple different ways, but when I refer to a wholetale transaction, I am referring to closing on the property using your own or a partner's resources and then reselling the property in the general marketplace. I will commonly make some minor improvements to the wholetale-transaction property to make it sell better. However, this is not a fix and flip situation in which I would hire a large number of contractors to make major layout and refinishing changes.

When I have a property that I decide fits the wholetale strategy, I will do one of two things:

1. Hire a person or two to clean up the property and do some painting so that the house is more presentable and will command a higher dollar in the retail market, as opposed to selling to an investor who would require a certain amount of equity in the deal to purchase it.

2. Fix a single major problem with the house, which was why I was able to buy it at a large discount. For example, replace a roof; replace some of the plumbing; or fix a kitchen or a bathroom.

You would be amazed at how much more equity and bottom-line profit you can keep when you close on the deal yourself and do minor work that takes less than a week. This is the key! We aren't looking to close and use these as fix and flip properties because, more often than not, there isn't enough profit or equity in the deal to warrant a full rehab. However, we can clean the property up, make it more presentable, and sell to the general market.

The beautiful part about wholetale transactions is that they are quick, require minimal capital investment, and have very little risk because you make your profit on the "buy." Now, how do we want to sell these properties? We want to sell them creatively so that we can profit for a long time! We want to sell these properties to retail buyers who either don't want to get a traditional loan or don't have the ability to get a traditional loan from a bank or other lender. There is a large market of people looking for owner-financed properties wherein the seller of the property will hold the note so that they can pay over time. We want to welcome these people into our business.

This is an opportune way to create larger and larger monthly income streams for free. When you purchase a wholetale-style property, there is a great chance that if you negotiated a good enough deal on the "buy," you can resell the property, getting your original purchase price as a down payment from the new buyer. Then you will receive the remaining amount they owe you in monthly installments. Much as in the case studies above, if you receive your original purchase price as a down payment, you will have an investment that will pay you for years to come, with minimum risk. I provide an example below:

Market value of house: $100,000

Purchase price: $25,000

Light repairs: $2,500

Total investment: $27,500

Resale price: $100,000

Down payment from new buyer: $30,000

Immediate profit of $2,500 (= $30,000 - $27,500)

Monthly payments on $70,000, financed by you, the seller, over 10 years @7% interest = $813.

Total income over the 10 years, including interest is $97,531 (= $813 x 12 x 10).

You just profited an extra $27,531 (= $97,231 - $70,000 owed) in interest income by financing the property for the buyer.

You just made over $30,000 more than what the property was worth by structuring your deal this way and locating the right buyer with the right situation and resources. Now tell me how many times will it take doing this before your lifestyle is improved?

Want to hear the next best part about this? You will enjoy tax benefits by selling on terms because you will only need to include the amount you earn on the property each year and not your total gain on the property as one bulk payment.

As mentioned earlier in the book, you need to become familiar with the laws and regulations in your area regarding owner financing. You can use owner financing in multiple ways with different buyers, but it is best to check with a local real estate attorney beforehand so that you can structure your deals in a legal fashion. Putting together a plan in any business prior to proceeding is always wise, but when providing great values to people and creating a great experience, you will limit your risk exposure.

To sell a property on terms, you simply communicate your goals and all necessary information to your title company or closing attorney so that they can create the mortgage, insurance, lien position, and promissory note for you. After this, you are ready to repeat the process!

If you are wondering why I don't close on these properties and completely fix and flip them, it is because of the extended exposure, capital investment, and inherent risk. Many times there will be properties that you can resell with minimal cleaning and fixing, earning the same amount of profit as you would by completely fixing and updating the property because a full renovation requires extra capital investment. Would you rather profit $30,000 with $25,000 invested and less than a week of renovations or profit $35,000 with $75,000 invested and 60 days of renovations?

**GREAT QUESTION: AM I MAXIMIZING MY EFFORTS BY CLOSING ON DEALS THAT I HAVE THE ABILITY TO FIX AND RESELL AT A GREAT PRICE TO CAPTURE MORE PROFITS AND EQUITY?**

# STEP THREE
# Retail Paper/Owning Debt

We have discussed the benefits of owning debt and including promissory notes in our business plan. We have covered how owning more and more debt as opposed to owing more and more debt is beneficial to our future and our financial freedom. Now let's discuss the different options we have for owning debt and working to build our paper portfolio.

Did you know you could wholesale notes? Were you aware that besides creating promissory notes by selling a property that you either own or own an interest in on terms, you can purchase notes at a discount? We have the ability to act like banks when and if we choose.

Not all notes are created equal. There are all different kinds of situations and circumstances surrounding each note and/or piece of debt. There are performing, non-performing, short-term, long-term, high-interest, and low-interest notes, and they vary in terms of risk, depending on the level of due diligence completed, among other factors.

Consider two different notes that are currently for sale. One of the notes is being sold by a traditional lending institution while the other is being sold by an investor. The institutional-quality note had the highest level of due diligence completed, and the borrower passed credit and financial checks, including proving long-standing income in his or her current career or job. The other note was created by a seller who was struggling to sell a house in a traditional fashion at a price he wanted. The investor created a note and lien position with a borrower who couldn't get a loan from a traditional lender and had recently changed jobs. Which note do you see as having more risk? Which note would you need to purchase at a larger discount to ensure your profitability over time? Have you thought about your ability to resell that note in the future? These are just a couple of factors you need to consider when you want to invest and create cashflow by building a paper(note) portfolio.

Non-performing notes are just as they sound. Non-performing. This means that, for whatever reason, the borrower has stopped making payments on the debt that the noteholder is attempting to sell. In this scenario it is important to do your due diligence and examine the situation in depth. What are the terms of the agreement? What is the difference between what is owed on the note and the value of the property? What is the borrower's situation? Does the borrower occupy the property? Have there been foreclosure attempts in the past? How long has the payment been delinquent? What lien position does the debt have? The more details you can uncover, the better feel you can get regarding whether or not you can protect a possible investment in the note.

A common strategy when investing in a non-performing note is to purchase the note at a deep discount, well below what is owed on the principle and well below the market value of the property that secures the note, and attempt to work with the borrower to get him or her to resume making payments. If this doesn't work, the new debt owner can begin the foreclosure process in order to take control of the property and resell it. Under this scenario, the debt owner may be able to capitalize and profit from his or her investment in the note when the property is sold. If the new noteholder is able to convince the original borrower to resume payments, the noteholder may earn substantial profits from the interest, principal, and possibly even late fee payments he or she will receive since the noteholder purchased the note at such a deep discount. The beautiful part about this is that the borrower gets to stay in the home, or keep the property in question, and not have to deal with the foreclosure process. Quicker and cleaner for everyone, with great upside.

Performing notes are debts that are currently in good standing and performing as planned. These notes can also sometimes be purchased at a discount, and it's still important to collect as much data as possible just as with the non-performing notes. Performing notes are commonly sold in order to obtain funds for reinvestment in another asset. It is common for both banks and investors to sell notes, even when they are performing as expected. A performing note with good due diligence performed on the borrower is typically ranked as a higher-quality, lower-risk note that can be sold at a premium. These are also generally easier to resell if you want to liquidate them in the future.

Notes are for sale as readily as houses and buildings are. You would be amazed at how you will find notes you can purchase if you retarget your marketing to mention notes and debt rather than just property. Joining local networking groups, using Craigslist ads, and posting on social media are all great ways to find opportunities to invest in debt.

We have discussed in detail how important it is to continue growing your network consistently. By doing so with notes in mind, you will realize how much opportunity there is for matching note sellers with note buyers, enabling you to profit by being the middleman. You can help put the two pieces together and take a piece of the pie, just as you do when wholesaling a traditional property. There is great opportunity within this sector that many miss out on because they don't know it's there! Based on my experience, noteholders are much quieter than property owners. This is a great advantage for you because you can become the eyes and ears for others looking for opportunity.

So, how do we wholesale a note? It's just like property! You locate investors who want to purchase notes and pair them with holders of notes that fit their criteria. If a buyer wants a $1^{st}$ lien position with "X" amount of interest and principal, then you know who to talk to when you come across paper that fits the bill.

Once you bring the two parties together, you can negotiate your cut. You can have an agreement drawn up to complete the transfer just as you do when wholesaling property. Talk with your closing attorney or title company to see if they need anything specific in your area, but in my experience, it has been an extremely simple and straightforward deal, with the title company or closing attorney handling the paperwork and transfer. What if you are able to negotiate a part of the cashflow from the note with the note buyer as your finder's fee? Time-free monthly income for as long as the agreement states. Remember to be creative in helping others!

If you want to purchase notes for your own portfolio, it can be a great way to branch into investing without having any month-to-month responsibility that comes with structural investments and rental property. If you have available capital and are looking at real estate as a possible avenue of investment, you might consider focusing on real-estate backed notes. This will generate regular, repeat income, no matter what is happening with the property.

My closest friend began investing in real estate by purchasing a $20,000 note on a single-family property across the country from where he lived. He was able to negotiate a great set of terms. The borrower, who is an investor, makes interest-only monthly payments, even when the property isn't performing. This strategy has allowed my friend to transition into owning rental property of his own and even partnering to purchase multiple other properties. This was a great start to his real estate investment portfolio. I really feel that notes are one of the most overlooked opportunities within the niche.

**GREAT QUESTION: AM I CONSIDERING ALL AVENUES OF REAL ESTATE THAT MAY FIT MY STRATEGY?**

# STEP THREE
# Should I Rehab This Myself?

This singular question is one of the most important questions that you should ask yourself anytime that you are looking at a possible investment property. All too often I see people wholesale a property for $5,000 when its upside potential is $50,000, just because they are afraid to take on the renovation project. Weigh the options before simply giving away opportunity and equity.

I will teach you how to rank different strategies in order to decide the best route to take with each property in the next step, but first you must understand that if you are looking at wholesaling a property with a larger spread, you need to be aware of the opportunity that you are forgoing.

You have already done the difficult part by locating and negotiating a possible great deal. Sometimes passing it on to someone else will make more sense, but by keeping an open mind and asking yourself the question, *Should I rehab this myself?* you may find you can increase your profit potential on each lead.

Never pass on an opportunity because you are afraid of the process. I feel so strongly about this that I will give you a couple principles you can use to help ease your fears and protect you from issues I myself have experienced and have had to overcome because I was acting inappropriately.

I look back at the deals that I have passed to other investors for single payments that make me shake and wince in a bit of pain. On one hand I did a great job of locating and negotiating killer deals. On the other hand, I gave the boat away for far too little because I didn't understand what the next steps in a renovation or rehab process really were. So, first and foremost, realize you are doing a great job of creating great deals, and don't be afraid to be a part of them!

Secondly, assemble your renovation team before your next project. Begin networking and ask for referrals and recommendations. It is common that a team of just a couple people will far exceed your expectations. This is especially true when you do a good job of communicating with them and taking care of them. I myself have gone through a whole slew of different skilled workers, and I can say that now that I apply these principles, I have, without a doubt, the best crew I have ever known

When dealing with skilled workers, make sure to set proper expectations and write absolutely everything down. More often than not these team members will be looking to follow your lead regarding what needs done and what the design is. You need your team members to perform their specific roles, not jump back and forth from one task to another. At no point should a carpenter become a designer choosing wall colors. You, your team members, and your specific role players need to be doing exactly what they are best at. If you aren't good at designing--which you probably aren't--sorry, you need to spend the couple hundred dollars and hire a designer. All too often investors want to save, save, save, and what they end up doing is "saving" $200 on a designer but losing $20,000 in the selling price when the renovation has been completed because the house doesn't fit current trends.

When you put everything in writing in the agreement, including a proper bid, there is no room for opinions and/or a change of plans by the renovation team members. This eliminates any surprises that cost more than expected. They are assigned specific jobs, and you pay accordingly so that you can create more opportunity with them and help provide more for them and their families because they provide a great service to yours.

Have the money ready to pay your team! You would be amazed at how much this helps the process. I hate when I see others hold out on paying or try to negotiate lower prices after the job is done. This doesn't build a strong relationship, and, worse, gives you a poor reputation. Have the money ready to pay the team when they complete the job at hand.

Hire a team that understands the renovation process and the order of operations. When a property is being renovated, there is a specific order of operations that needs to be followed. You don't put down new flooring and then have the framing, dry walling, and painting done, requiring new workers to traipse across your brand-new floor all day. You don't necessarily need to discuss every step in great detail, but it's important that your team understand the order of operations. If you have to worry about operations all day, you can't focus on more important things, like the direction of the business, and that's not good for anyone. So, hire trusted workers!

These steps may seem simple, but they are all too easily overlooked. If you follow these steps, you will be able to maximize your profit on every lead and opportunity. Following these steps will allow you to build a flourishing business that can provide for others and create great opportunities for future buyers, tenants, or investors. People want to work with someone who is organized and understands the importance of quality work.

---

## GREAT QUESTION: AM I PASSING ON OPPORTUNITY OUT OF FEAR?

---

# STEP THREE
# Rental Property

Rental property is one of the single greatest makers of millionaires over the past century. As discussed previously, the best, more profitable, long lasting, investors work in particular niches and have specific criteria, such as single-family homes, multifamily homes, commercial buildings, storage units, mobile home parks, etc. Remember, you need to establish a list of criteria for yourself and your company and stick to that criteria. This will limit your risk while also promoting growth and providing exponential reward.

It is impossible for me to develop a list of criteria that works for everyone in every market. It is important to do your research, network with other successful investors, and look within yourself to decide what strategy best fits your personality.

Understanding that there is a myriad of different directions to take in the real estate industry is essential. There are endless ways that you can design profitable deals by solving problems for others and structuring transactions that work for both parties. I discuss a few of these in detail below to give you an idea of some options for using property to build a flourishing portfolio in a manner that best fits you. No matter how you choose to acquire property, it is important to understand there is typically more than one way to look at a situation, and these different ways lend themselves to different solutions and types of closings.

1. **Traditional purchase:** This is the most common real estate transaction, wherein an investor or buyer purchases a property

with his or her own cash, credit, or resources. Banks and traditional lenders are used for these purchases, and closing times can range from a few days to a few weeks, depending on available funds and loan requirements. Most people never consider anything beyond this type of transaction. Upon completion of the transaction, the property is in the buyer's name.

2. **Subject To:** This type of transaction is used to make an offer "subject to" the current debt on the property. The buyer's goal here is to solve a problem for the seller by taking over responsibility for the monthly debt service to capture either equity or monthly cashflow. In this scenario the seller's debt remains in his or her name, while ownership of the property is transferred to the new buyer. There is the risk that the bank or lender may enforce what is called the "due on sale" clause wherein the debt is required to be paid in full upon the change in ownership. To avoid this, it is very important to stay current on all monthly payments so that the bank is satisfied each month. Be aware of this risk and plan for the possibility of the clause being enforced, even though that is rare. When this transaction is executed, the buyer becomes the owner of the property while the seller's name remains on the debt.

3. **Lease Option:** This is a creative way to control a property before taking ownership. The seller retains ownership of the property for a certain period of time, while the buyer leases the property from the seller with a right to "master lease" the property. This means the buyer can sub-lease the property to other tenants to create a spread in rent. For example, a buyer may lease the property for $500 per month and sublease it (re-rent to another tenant) for $750 a month, profiting $250 a month on the deal. During the lease period the buyer has an option to purchase the property, which means the seller can sell the property only to this buyer until the option expires or fails to be exercised. Check your local markets for rules and regulations on lease options; not every state plays by the same set of rules. Upon exercise of the option, the property is transferred into the buyer's name. Prior to the option exercise, the property remains in the name of the seller.

4. **Assumption:** Similar to a "subject to" transaction the buyer in this scenario is looking to purchase a property for the amount of the debt owed, but in this scenario the buyer assumes the debt ownership, meaning the loan will be transferred into the name of the buyer, and the seller no longer has to worry that the buyer will default on the payments and affect his/her (the seller's) credit rating since the debt doesn't remain in his/her name. The buyer must qualify for the debt in place in this scenario, which, more times than not, results in the debt being paid off, and a more traditional transaction ensues. Upon completion, the property is in the buyer's name.

5. **Owner Finance/Seller Carryback:** Here the seller of the property "carries" the note. This means that the seller becomes the bank and holds the note; thus, the buyer makes monthly payments to the seller. The note is secured by the property, and the seller has a lien position. The buyer is responsible for making monthly payments. Depending on the negotiated terms, the buyer may have the potential to trade rent for monthly debt payments, while capturing possible equity and appreciation. Seller carryback is a term occasionally used for a strategy involving a lender, with the seller "carrying" a specific amount of the purchase price and a bank or other lender providing the remainder of the purchase price. In this instance, the seller has a second lien position, and the buyer has two monthly debt payments. This strategy is used to avoid using any money out-of-pocket; instead, the buyer is using 100% of other people's money to invest in property, using traditional bank methods. Upon completion of the transaction, the property is in the buyer's name.

6. **Private Money/Hard Money:** Private money and hard money are two different funding sources. Many believe they are the same but, in truth, they are different. Private money is money that you have available to you due to building relationships and trust over time with friends, family, colleagues, and other investors. Not everyone has access to this money. This capital is available to you specifically in many cases. Hard money is money that is available to the general public. This type of capital is typically used for

shorter-term investments and flip-style properties and transactions as opposed to longer-term investments and cashflow assets. Hard money is usually more expensive as well, with interest rates in the teens, not including origination and paperwork fees. (Origination fees are the cost of doing business, and the cost associated with creating the lending opportunity.) The benefit to using private money is that you typically have more flexibility since you have better relationships with the lenders; thus, they are usually more understanding than a bank or hard money lender.

The purpose of owning rentals is to grow wealth, time-freedom, cashflow, and options, and create flexibility in your business. Any one of the above-mentioned strategies can be used, depending on state and local regulations, and any one of these strategies can be implemented successfully when applied in the correct manner. If one of these strategies fits your internal identity, it's best to focus on that strategy specifically until you reach a point wherein diversifying or scaling will allow you to grow your portfolio and your opportunities. Too many people want to go from $50,000 per year in income to $1,500,000 in income and think they have failed if they don't hit that mark. In reality, just a couple of rental properties structured in the correct way can change your financial life.

To complete the above-mentioned transactions, you need to establish a relationship with a reliable title company or closing attorney who can prepare the appropriate documents for you, as discussed in Step One. More often than not, the exact same purchase agreement can be used for all the strategies, accompanied by a separate document or agreement to solidify the remaining details. For example, I can use the same basic "For Sale By Owner" purchase agreement for both a traditional transaction and a seller-financed deal, but with the seller-financed transaction, I attach a separate sheet explaining the terms of the deal, and the title company takes care of the rest for us. This is truly what you need to have so that you can focus on being creative and not on things outside your realm of expertise. Remember we want to focus on one thing! So, let's make sure you are focused on building a million-dollar business, not a paper-organizing, time-consuming, side-work company that doesn't earn any extra income regardless of who prepares the documents.

## GREAT QUESTION: DOES THIS PROPERTY FIT MY CRITERIA?

# STEP FOUR
# Ranking the Exit Strategies to Choose Best Possible Offer

When we begin ranking the best possible solutions and strategies is when things get exciting! This is the step in which you begin to see potential profits and different deal structures that enable you to be paid over and over again for providing a solution to someone's problem. It is important that we are ranking multiple different strategies, as discussed previously, because there will be times where multiple strategies will work, but one of them will involve the least risk, least capital investment, and creates the most profit. These are the strategies and solutions that we want to focus on and build our offers around.

To organize your strategies and pair the one that best fits your identity and that of your present possible seller, you need to comprehend the long-term gains and effects of the transaction. For example, if the seller has a debt issue and must get the debt out of his or her name in order to borrow money to purchase another property, a "subject to" offer isn't going to work. This is an example in which the transaction would be a great win for you, the buyer, but less than satisfactory for the seller. Thus, the deal will never work, and that results in zero profit every time. So, first things first! Make sure you are pairing a solution with the actual problem at hand and not just presenting a solution that looks great on paper for you.

Secondly, you need to estimate the amount of profit you expect from the specific deal. Are you expecting to flip this property at a specific purchase price due to the amount of equity in it, or are you planning to hold onto this property for the long-term cashflow possibilities? Once you answer this question, you can narrow your options down even further. If you are going to be holding the property long term, you want the best possible price and loan terms on any money that you borrow so that your monthly cashflow is as high as possible. Thus, in more cases than not, a hard money loan would not be a great choice, but using your own capital, seller financing, or private-lender funds would work great.

Let's work through a comprehensive example together to illustrate. This is a property and scenario that I actually experienced. I mentioned this property earlier in the building value example, but now I will walk you through my thought process as I ranked strategies and exit plans in order to choose the most profitable one. On the surface, this deal looked like a clean and simple fix-and-flip, using private money so that I needed to use zero out-of-pocket to make a quick and easy $40,000. However, when I stepped back and gave it some thought, I uncovered better scenarios.

We had the opportunity to purchase this specific property for $50,000 when the house was worth closer to $100K or $110K after being cleaned up and painted. Light cosmetic work would have given us a profit of roughly $40,000, using private funds to cover the entire transaction, including the remodeling. Cut and dried, right? Wrong!

Let's take a step back and consider the seller's scenario. The seller's father had been moved into a nursing home, and his assets needed to be sold to fund his health care. Knowing this situation and understanding the seller's need for capital, would a "subject to" offer, wherein the current debt remains in the name of the seller, make sense? No. Good answer!

The seller needs money and can't keep the debt. Would assuming the mortgage make sense? No. The seller still wouldn't have the money needed; the debt would just no longer be in the seller's name. That option is out.

What about a lease option? We could rent the property for a while, cover any debts, and put a little monthly income in the seller's pocket. Would this have helped the seller with sizeable nursing home payments? No, probably

# IF YOU CAN'T CASHFLOW AFTER THIS

not. Let's pass on that offer.

We could purchase the property in a traditional fashion, using a traditional bank loan. This type of closing will take up to 45 days. Does this work for the seller? Possibly, but then we bear the risk that the house doesn't pass the inspections, depending on the type of loan we want. Moreover, it may create a scenario in which the seller decides to list the property and create more awareness. This isn't our best scenario. It's not win-win for us or the seller, who will have longer to wait for the needed capital. Remember, we have some time stressors, given the need to pay the father's nursing home bills.

Well, we have an easy $40 to $50k in equity for a flip. We could use hard money and give the seller the $50,000. This would certainly solve the seller's problem. It would get her the needed capital quickly. All her responsibility for the property would be relieved, and she could move on. Not a bad choice! What is the downside? Hard money is expensive, and if we find any other issues or surprises, our bottom-line profit would rapidly begin to shrink. How else could we make this work quickly, but make it more affordable or profitable?

We could wholesale the property to another buyer. That would get the seller the cash needed, and we would profit with minimum risk. A viable option, but this is a great deal. We have done the hard work and need to reap the rewards. We need to close on this deal ourselves.

So, to make this win-win, the seller needs the $50,000 in proceeds, and we need to fund the deal in the most affordable fashion. Our two choices are now to use private funds or our own capital.

Private funds may cost us a few thousand dollars on a flip scenario, which is certainly more affordable than the hard money. The seller will receive her $50,000, and we can flip the property. But maybe we want to keep the property because on closer inspection, the property fits our criteria to a tee! This two-bedroom, one-bath house is ranch-style, with a full basement, new mechanicals, new roof, and new siding. Given it's only a two-bedroom structure, the $50,000 in private money debt service would be a little expensive since rent on a two-bedroom in that area is only $750 a month.

So, private money is a good choice, but not a great choice. What if. . .just, what if? As it turned out, we used our own capital, so we had no debt service. We added a 3rd bedroom in the basement and raised the rent to $1,100 per month. This gave us the option to resell the property for a higher price, enabling us to recapture our original investment and earn a profit on top of it. Or we could hang onto the property as a rental. We could rent it for $1,100 a month, and when we are ready, we can go to the bank, pull our investment out, and buy more houses. NOW THAT IS A WIN-WIN!

We have long-term options. We have long-term income. We have our own capital invested in a tangible asset that produces income for us every month, and we have the ability to borrow against the property and reuse our money. We kept our private money and hard money options open for future projects that might work better, and we have also cured the seller's problem by giving her $50,000 for the house, which can be used for the father's health care. This is a perfect scenario now. We have created both options and income for ourselves, while bumping our net worth and cashflow.

Do you see how this transaction took multiple turns and twists, and how I weighed multiple different options? This is what's possible when you begin pairing real solutions with real problems and understand what the deal may look like a few months down the road versus just today, in this moment.

We went from a for-sure fix and flip (wholetale style, given that it needed only a light cosmetic clean-up), borrowing money, and selling it as a two-bedroom, one-bath house to creating $1,100 per month income for ourselves, using our own resources, and owning a three-bedroom, one-and-a-half bath house for very little additional investment. Furthermore, we could sell it for a much higher price if we chose to do so in the future, or we could also borrow against it to buy more property.

This is how wealth is built. We just turned one house into a possible three, with the same amount of capital invested, creating monthly cashflow from thin air and exchanging a lump sum payment for monthly income that could possibly be as high as $3,000 after future house purchases. Not bad! Examine each option in detail!

When examining the various scenarios, you will find that some may be more profitable, but will involve more risk than you are comfortable with, so you will end up choosing the smaller-profit option in exchange for peace of mind. This is perfectly fine! This is your investor identity right now, and it's okay to start slow and grow with time. You will also see situations in which you can rank certain scenarios and properties with different profitability levels. You will learn that it may make sense to wholesale a property to a retail buyer instead of purchasing it as a fix and flip. It may cost $75,000 to buy and $25,000 to fix in order to sell it for $150,000, generating a $50,000 profit. Alternatively, you could sell the property at a discount to a retail buyer who can make the property his or her own and does not need the equity an investor needs. Thus, you can sell your $75,000 contract to the retail buyer for $125,000, generating the same $50,000 profit for yourself with no risk and in less time. Which strategy would you choose in that situation? I know which one I would. You can only do this by examining each scenario in detail and mapping out the long-term effects of each.

---

**GREAT QUESTION: AM I LOOKING AT THIS PROBLEM FROM MULTIPLE PERSPECTIVES AND PAIRING THE MOST PROFITABLE SOLUTION TO IT WHILE UNDERSTANDING THE LONG-TERM CONSEQUENCES OF MY ACTIONS?**

---

## STEP FOUR
# PUTTING THE OFFER ON THE TABLE

The only way you can ever close a deal is to make offers! Terrifying, I know. I promise it will become easier over time, and after reading this section, you will understand that you will be presenting the best possible scenario for relieving the seller's pain, and that it is up to the seller to accept your help. It is your job to educate and provide the solution. You will never convince someone to see something your way unless they are open to receiving help.

The material in this section was covered in the first installment of this series (*If You Can't Wholesale After This... I've Got Nothing For You*) in Step 5 on page 74, but this time we're covering it from a different angle. We are no longer exclusively looking at and making offers on properties that our buyers want to own. We want to own these properties, and we have multiple solutions to provide. We need to do so in a manner that allows our seller to choose which works best for him or her.

I am a big believer in making your offers in person. I understand that there are times in which "in person" isn't realistic or possible. In these situations, communicating with the seller on the phone, at the very least, will help create a better atmosphere that facilitates conversation and negotiation. It is too easy for a seller to disappear when you send a text message or email and your message is taken in the wrong context, or the seller doesn't understand the offer you're proposing. Being open and available typically creates the best scenario and will help raise your conversion rate.

Our number one job when presenting an offer to a seller is to educate the seller on the process and to always, always, always... Always... (did I mention always?) provide a solution to his or her problem! If your offer doesn't provide a real solution to the seller's problem, the answer will be "no" every single time, and you will have wasted your and everyone else's time. Please keep this in mind. The sure-fire way to eliminate any chance of a deal coming together is failing to provide a solution. Thus, we want to focus on this first and foremost.

Our second job is to present our multiple potential solutions in a simple fashion that will allow the seller to decide which one works best for him or her. Many call this presentation sheet a "letter of intent." While non-binding, the letter of intent allows the seller to select from one of multiple options. Our most successful letters of intent typically provide three possible solutions to the problem, and we ask the seller to choose which works best for him or her. Once the seller chooses which would work best, I further educate the seller on what that choice will mean for him/her now and in the long run. This lays everything in front of them, making our offer as transparent as possible to avoid any future confusion.

When designing your offer, whether verbal or written, you need to communicate your letter of intent in very clear, concise, simple terminology. If at any point the seller becomes confused regarding your offer, the seller will default to "no." This is true when you're selling anything. If you need to persuade someone to improve her life, you need to do so in a manner that she will be open to and understand. Be confident in your offer. Remember you have exercised due diligence in order to come up with the best possible solutions for your sellers and that when they choose the best option for them, you will perform, and everyone will be leaving the table better off.

When you present your offers, present them with open ears. Educate the sellers on the options you're providing and then be quiet! Let them think. Let them choose. Let them ask questions. I have observed newbie investors present an offer and then continue talking the entire time, or for 10 minutes after they have finished presenting the options, giving the seller no time to think or make a decision. Present your offer and shut up!

Once you've presented your offer, realize that there is no secret sauce that will convert every deal or offer. You are inevitably going to hear "no" more than you hear "yes" but as long as you understand that you provided the best possible win-win solution for both you and them, you should feel good about what you are doing. Stay consistent and stay hungry. It will happen. All it takes is one "yes."

---

**GREAT QUESTION: DO I FEEL GOOD ABOUT THE SOLUTIONS I PROVIDED?**

---

# STEP FOUR
# Ask Them How You Can Best Serve

This extremely important question deserves an entire section of its own. The two most significant questions you can ask in both real estate and life in general are as follows:

1. "Why?"

2. "How can I best serve you?"

If you ask these two questions when you are learning about the seller and when you are presenting your offers, you will increase your productivity and close-rate beyond your wildest dreams.

These two questions will suggest the best possible solutions to sellers' problems and will provide a singular impetus for sellers to give you property under the right situations. I have had properties literally given to me because the pain was so great that when I asked, "How can I best serve you?" they responded that I could best help by taking over the responsibility of the house.

Ask this question! Always! You are here to serve and improve others' lives. To do this you must ask them how you can best serve them so that you can build offers that fit their needs. This single question will unlock the seller's true motivation, the best possible solutions, and reveal how to best pair the two so that you can close more deals with more satisfied sellers.

The relational building tool of this specific question cannot be overstated. This single question is crucial to your success!

**GREAT QUESTION: HOW CAN I BEST SERVE YOU?**

## STEP FOUR
# Explaining the Problem-Solving Process

When you provide multiple solutions to your sellers and they are open to one or more of the solutions, you can begin to explain the actual problem-solving process. No matter what solution the sellers have chosen, this is when you should educate them further on their choice and also on the next steps needed to move forward, such as signing a purchase agreement, signing separate terms or agreement documents, and communicating with the title company or closing attorney.

Your explanations should be simple, straightforward, and to the point. The more you get off track, the more grey area you introduce into the situation over the coming days and weeks. At this point you want to explain the timeline and the next steps that they need to take.

The order in which all this should happen will follow a timeline similar to the one below:

1. Choose solution.
2. Agree on terms.
3. Sign purchase agreement and supporting documents that are supplied by local title company or attorney.
4. Explain next steps for closing.

5. Make copies of agreements and send to title company/ attorney.

6. Let seller know typical timeline for closing.

7. Provide contact information and let seller know the times you are available to answer questions ... NOT 24/7!

8. Reassure seller of your performance record and tell seller that you look forward to helping him/her through this specific process.

9. Part ways.

10. Stay in contact throughout closing process to keep relationship and confidence strong.

Keep it this simple. When you keep things simple when explaining the process, you set a tone for quick, smooth closings. This will go a long way toward eliminating potential chaos, not only for your business, but for the title company and your own sanity. This easy step will help establish a long-term growing and glowing reputation for you, your business, and the company with whom you associate. Guess where most referrals come from? That's right, past sellers, and when we are focused on long-term cashflow, it takes only a few referrals to make a big difference in our lives.

I hope you are starting to realize how close you really are to making a large impact in your financial life.

---

**GREAT QUESTION: AM I KEEPING THINGS SIMPLE FOR EVERYONE INVOLVED AND EXPLAINING THINGS IN A CLEAR, CONCISE MANNER THAT ALLOWS EVERYONE AMPLE TIME TO VOICE HIS OR HER THOUGHTS?**

---

**STEP FIVE**
# Accepted Offer Next Action Steps

---

We have an accepted offer! Fantastic! Now we are ready to take the next steps in our process and get ready to close the deal. At this point we have a set plan for closing and the type of transaction that we plan to use. Depending on the type of transaction, we may have slightly different tasks to complete, such as contacting lenders, inspectors, or other investors, but our process from here on out is very similar regardless of the deal.

Our first responsibility will be to make copies of our purchase agreement and give them to our seller and our title company or closing attorney. At this point we are waiting to hear back from the title company to learn if there is anything more we need to do. They will provide us with clear action steps if there are any tasks specifically for us. Most of the time the title company/closing attorney will no longer need us, but occasionally they may ask for assistance or clarity on our purchase agreements.

This is also the point at which we will confirm the name in which we will be taking title to the property—such as an LLC (Limited Liability Company) or a trust--with the title company or attorney. Many investors put property into land trusts to help protect them against future lawsuits or liability due to unforeseen issues or claims. The best approach is to speak to a real estate attorney in your local market to devise a plan that best protects you and your business.

In addition to sending documents to the seller and title company, you will need to organize your resources to prepare for closing. If you are using private money or hard money, you will need to send those agreements to the title company so that the title company can prepare any necessary promissory notes and record the lien positions to protect your investors. If the purchase agreement involved any earnest money, you will need to send a check to the title company for the escrow account. NEVER send earnest money to a seller or any party other than the title company or closing attorney working the specific deal. If you do so, you risk losing that money because there is nothing to keep the seller from running with your money at this point.

Typically, the private money lender or hard money lender will send the requisite funds directly to the title company. The title company or attorney will inform them of the exact amount due. It works the same way if you are using your own funds, too. The title company informs you of the amount owed, and you send the money directly to them.

Once you have your resources organized, you should alert your team, along with any contractors or skilled workers you'll be using for renovations, so that they will be ready to begin work if anything is needed immediately upon closing. The longer a property sits vacant, the more costly the purchase becomes, and the more risk you face due to things such as damage, rising holding costs, and... squatters.

At this point your biggest responsibility is relaying information to and from the title company or seller in a timely manner if required. If not, you are ready for closing day! There may be other small miscellaneous items to take care of, given that each deal is slightly different, but this is the general order of preparing for closing.

———

**GREAT QUESTION: IS THERE ANY WAY THAT I OR MY TEAM CAN HELP SMOOTH OUT THE PROCESS BETWEEN THE SIGNING OF THE PURCHASE AGREEMENT AND CLOSING DAY?**

———

## STEP FIVE
# Can I Create Monthly Income for Free?

During this stage of the process I am asking myself if there is a way I can create a line of free income before or immediately following closing. If the property doesn't fit my specific holding criteria exactly, I will consider reselling on terms, creating a note for myself, while requiring a down payment that will be enough to cover my initial purchase price.

If this happens to be the case, I inform the title company that I am planning on an immediate resale, but let them know I will close on the property, regardless, so that they will continue the current process. There are times when I have so many interested parties that I could wholesale the property, paying for it with a promissory note, and there are other times in which it makes more sense to close on the property and resell it to a retail buyer looking for a seller-financed deal. It all depends on the deal and how the numbers break down in combination with the risk/reward factors that we discussed in the previous steps.

When creating a free line of income by selling before your closing date, you need to disclose it to your seller and assure him or her that the closing will still happen as planned, but that you will have a partner closing on the property in his or her company name instead of yours. Each party will also sign off on your profits. This is good because it creates transparency via the disclosures designed to protect all parties. This transaction just becomes an assignment of contract, with the terms of the contract listing any initial and monthly payment responsibilities of the end buyer. This is a rare occurrence, to say the least. Most of the time at this stage you will be closing on the property yourself and then reselling it for a down payment and monthly terms. Nevertheless, I wanted to let you know of this possibility in the event that you are presented with this situation. Communication with the title company at this point is the key.

When selling on owner-financed terms using a promissory note, the transaction takes place as a normal sale to a retail buyer looking for an owner-financed opportunity, and you will follow the steps discussed previously.

---

**GREAT QUESTION: CAN I CREATE A FREE LINE OF INCOME SUCH THAT I, OR MY INVESTORS, ARE CASHED OUT OF ALMOST IMMEDIATELY AFTER CLOSING?**

---

# STEP FIVE
# DO I NEED TO GATHER MORE RESOURCES?

I personally love asking myself this question as closing day approaches because it gets me in the mindset of checking off each task that needs to be completed prior to closing. Below is a short check list that will allow you to sleep easy at night, knowing you are ready for closing.

1. Paperwork signed and at title company:
   Yes or No

2. Funds allocated and ready to be sent in for closing:
   Yes or No

3. Seller is informed of closing date.
   Yes or No

4. All investors or partners are informed of property closing.
   Yes or No

5. General idea of best strategy to use on property?
   Yes or No

If you can answer yes to these five questions you are ready to close!

---

**GREAT QUESTION: AM I READY TO CLOSE?**

---

## STEP FIVE
# Setting Expectations with Title Company or Attorney

Setting expectations is a step commonly missed by investors and investing companies alike. It is a short step that simply establishes the goal and proposes a timeline for the transaction in question. When I send a purchase agreement to the title company/closing attorney, I make sure to explain my goals for the transaction as well as the goals of the seller. I let them know if the transaction is a traditional sale or a more creative deal, and I confirm that the proposed closing date is realistic if the contract depends on a quick closing. More times than not there are no issues, but by setting expectations and asking questions, you occasionally discover something that still needs to be done. If it requires you contact your seller, you can do so quickly and get the matter handled, rather than have the title company/attorney think you already have taken care of it when you haven't. This quick, simple, extra step helps everything move along slightly smoother than it otherwise might. Remember the title company and attorneys work hard for you; don't neglect to work hard for them!

**GREAT QUESTION: AM I PROVIDING THE BEST POSSIBLE EXPERIENCE FOR MY TITLE COMPANY?**

# STEP FIVE
# Understand Your Security and Lien Position

If you are selling the property on terms, you need to understand your lien position prior to closing. Liens have different positions, and these determine the order in which the lienholder gets paid if a borrower or homeowner defaults on the agreed upon terms.

A first lien is the most secure. When selling on terms to a buyer who is not also using a bank loan, you will typically be in first position. First position will be paid out anytime the property were to transfer names so that you are secure in your investment. This means that if the borrower were to default, you would be repaid in full prior to any lienholders with subordinate positions being paid anything.

Second position lienholders will receive payment only after the first lienholders are paid in full. This is a riskier position because if the property sells for less than the total of both liens, you won't receive the full amount owed to you since the first position lien must be completely satisfied first. Before you lend money in return for a subordinated lien position, consider the value of the property and the amount owed to the first lienholder. If the property is worth less than what is owed on the first position lien, don't lend the money!

There can be $3^{rd}$ lien positions, $4^{th}$, and so on. Each is subordinate to the higher-ranked (lower position) lien, and the more subordinate the lien, the riskier it is since the chances of getting paid from the proceeds of the sale of the property are very low. I personally recommend that you don't invest in a loan in which you would be taking anything more subordinate than a $2^{nd}$ lien, and that's assuming the value of the property is solid. Ideally you want to be in the $1^{st}$ spot if possible. Always confirm your position with the title company prior to closing so you have a clear understanding of your security and investment.

---

**GREAT QUESTION: WHAT LIEN POSITION DO I HOLD IN THIS DEAL, AND AM I SECURED IN BEING PAID WHAT I'M OWED FOR YEARS TO COME?**

---

# STEP FIVE
# Closing Day

The greatest day for everyone in the real estate business--closing day! No matter which side of the closing table you are on, your life and business are getting better. Whether you are selling for a profit, taking a loss to reduce mental stress and liquidate poor choices, buying a new asset, selling a contract, or anything in between, your life is getting better! The day of the closing is the one day to which every investor looks forward. So, how do we handle closing day? We just show up, right? Well, believe it or not, there are some best practices to follow. Let's cover a couple quick points that will ensure closing day goes as planned.

Something my team and I like to do on closing day is contact the other party involved, whether it be a seller, buyer, or investor, to remind them it was an honor to deal with them and to thank them for their time and cooperation. This has literally saved us deals in the past.

If you have been investing for any amount of time, closing multiple deals, you will have undoubtedly dealt with someone who gets cold feet on closing day. It's a big move! Remember our timeline and the expectations we set? This should come as no big surprise because we understand that our other party is either elated, or nervous, and possibly a combination of the two.

Simply hearing from you or your team can ease these nerves because it makes the deal real again. It reminds them they are dealing with real people and honest performers, so it can remind them why they chose to work with you in the first place. Up until this point they may have heard from you and the team to some extent, but not at the same level.

Let me share a story. I once had a retail buyer for a property that I was selling outright for cash. The young man had made a great choice. He was buying a house below market rate. He was gaining equity. He had taken the time and had the discipline to save up enough money to buy the house outright. He did everything right. There was only one problem. It was his FIRST house!

If you have ever bought a house, can you remember your first time? Did you want to throw up? Exactly! It was the same for this gentleman, and on closing day those feelings were stronger than ever. This once smooth deal was becoming a rocky one, at best. He felt paralyzed at the thought of going to the bank to get a cashier's check or wiring the funds. (This was back when you could still pay with a check in Ohio.) He called the title company and told them he was thinking about passing on the deal because it was too painful. The title company called me, and our team gave him a ring.

Fifteen minutes later he was on his way to the bank. What did we say, you ask? We asked this:

> "Hey, how can we help?"

That's what it took. That simple question reminded him that we were in this together and that he had chosen to work with us because we were real and honest. He had done great. He would have equity. He would have options. He had the money. He had done alright for himself at an age that others would dream about! We didn't want him to lose out on that opportunity because it was uncomfortable.

We ended up closing the deal that day, and the buyer contacted us a few months later to let us know that he was happy with the choice, and he thanked us for everything. Without the closing day call, this deal may have fallen apart, and he may have lost out on a free and clear house with big upside potential.

Contacting the parties involved is our first and most important task on closing day. Our second is double-checking the funding. It should already be in place, but it is best to make one last contact, confirm terms and agreements, ask for any last-second questions, and then move forward.

This sets us up for success, and then our last duty is to be on time with any documents or resources necessary, including LLC or company information, operating agreements, identifications, and anything else the title company or closing attorney may ask for upfront. Typically, the closing agent will alert you to what is needed before closing so you don't have to panic and bring everything with you every time.

"CLOSED!"

Finally, after closing we are going to evaluate our experience and leave a review for the company that we have worked with. This will build a great relationship and will allow for even better transactions in the future. You nailed it!

So, that's it right!? Well, don't we want to do this again? Don't we want to scale? Don't we need to make sure our new investments actually pay us? Don't we want a large freedom building, flourishing business? Yes? Okay then this is what we do next!

## GREAT QUESTION: AM I CONSIDERING THE OTHER PARTY'S FEELINGS ON CLOSING DAY?

## STEP SIX
# WHAT TO EXPECT AFTER CLOSING

After closing, there are a few specific tasks that you and your team need to perform. Selling a property for a lump sum doesn't require much. Your only job is to give the new owner keys to the property if you haven't yet and wait for your wire/check. However, there are crucial steps that must be taken if the property you just purchased is vacant or needs work. If you sold a property on terms and plan to hold a note, there are important steps in that scenario as well. I provide the essential steps for these last two scenarios below:

Steps to take after purchasing a new property:

**Step 1.** Obtain keys from seller or closing agent and immediately secure the property. If the property currently has a tenant, the property should be secure, as is, and you need to make copies of that specific key. This will allow you to give keys to the necessary team members and have spares in case of a lost key.

If the property is vacant, you need to take the keys and immediately have the locks changed. You don't know who has extra sets of those keys, and your first job is to secure the property to prevent any damage or intruders. Have your team or skilled workers change the locks and have spares of the new keys made so you and your team are the only ones with keys to the property. You take an unnecessary risk and set yourself up for a possible loss by skipping this step. Never skip it! Remember my squatter house story?

That can happen to you!

**Step 2.** If there is a tenant in place, you need to contact that person ASAP if he or she is unaware of the sale. We require the seller to contact any tenants prior to closing and even ask the seller to introduce us to them in some cases. This enables your team to get to know the current tenant(s). We also require all prior lease and tenant information documentation before closing. Sometimes this just isn't possible, though. As you will discover, not all landlords and property owners keep good records, and some don't keep any records at all. This is why they are having problems in the first place. I will teach you how to keep great records and secure yourself.

If the property is vacant, you will have changed the locks. There is a good chance the property will need some sort of maintenance or, at a minimum, cleaning before a tenant can be placed. Now is the time to contact any specialist or skilled workers you plan on hiring to do the work. We like to schedule this in advance so that these people are ready to go on closing day--or immediately following closing day--but these teams can be very busy, depending on the market, and you may need to wait until after closing to schedule them. Do so as soon as possible because the longer the property sits, the more expensive it becomes. Remember at this point our "asset" is a liability because it is only taking money from us until we get a tenant placed.

**Step 3.** If there is a tenant in place, you and your team should decide whether or not you plan on keeping this tenant in place. If there is a lease agreement, you must abide by the lease until it expires. If you want to change the terms of the lease, you can negotiate a new lease with the tenant(s) if you are interested in keeping them, or you can review their lease to make sure they aren't in violation of any of the terms. If they are, you have grounds to remove them; if not, it will more than likely be best to keep the tenant in place and collect the rent payments until their lease is up. If the property is rented for less than current values, you can inform the tenant that the rent will increase when a new lease is signed. If the tenant meets your intake requirements, which I will be discussing soon, then great! If not, it will be best to move on and find someone who better fits the property.

If the tenant will be remaining in the property for any amount of time during which a rent payment is due, you will need to set the expectations regarding where and how the rent is to be sent and collected. You do not want to have to have team members go to the property to collect rent. The tenant needs to be responsible for paying the rent on time, be it in person, via mail, or electronically. If you plan on going to the property to collect rent, remember to ask yourself the great question I presented earlier: *What would my life look like if I had 50 or 100 more of these?* As you may imagine, if you have more than one or two tenants that you need to visit to collect rent, you will be wasting an outrageous amount of time that could be used on further growing your business. Don't allow this.

If the property is vacant, your team should complete any maintenance or renovations that need done to get the property either rent-ready or ready to resell on terms, if that is your game plan. Your role during this is to address any questions or needs that could hold up progress. It's best to have project managers in place to assist with anything needed so that you can continue to scale, but in the beginning, there is a good chance you will be wearing this hat. It requires you to provide funds, help purchase materials if need be, and/or assist in business-related roles, but you won't have any responsibility for physically completing the project. This is not your role!

Let me tell you something that Ben taught me very early on about paying for these services that saved me from a number of different possible losses. He referred to it as "getting ahead of each other." You don't want the workers "ahead" of you, and you don't want to be too far "ahead" of them. This means that you should not be paying for jobs in full at the outset, and you should always have the funds ready to make payment when the job is completed. There may be a small stipend required along the way, but overall the job should be completed before any major payment is made. This protects you from having jobs left unfinished. This is also good for the skilled worker or workers because it keeps them consistent in their work.

**Step 4.** If the property is occupied and the seller had previously received a security deposit from the tenant(s), you are owed that deposit. The title company or closing attorney will have added that to your funds. You should deposit it in a separate non-interest-bearing account to hold until the tenant moves out. You should also set up a separate business account to deposit incoming rent checks. This will be key for accounting and tracking rental income. In addition to having a separate business account, it is smart to have rent roll software. A rent roll keeps track of payments and payment dates. You can also have the deposit tracked with this to prove income. This will make your life easier, as well as that of your CPA and/or bookkeeper, when it comes to tax time. Some of this software is free, or you can pay for software with more features. Many people use software, such as Quickbooks, while others simply use Excel spreadsheets. Check with your CPA to determine which they prefer.

When the renovation has been completed on a vacant property, it is time to begin the process of marketing it for rent or sale. We will cover this more in depth in the next section, but you are now ready to move this liability into the asset column. It is best to track the expenses incurred during the renovation, i.e., materials and labor, as well since these expenses can be used in different ways to reduce your tax bill. Don't forget this!

**Step 5.** This step is taken when a tenant is moving out after purchase. This happens a lot. Inheriting tenants is tricky because you are typically inheriting some sort of problem. If the property and situation were perfect, the previous seller probably wouldn't have been selling, right? So, if the tenant is moving out, that is perfectly fine.

It is important to understand the process of a move-out. You want to have as much notice as possible from the tenant. Require 30 days if possible. Also require them to contact you upon move-out to return the keys so that you can secure your property ASAP and don't risk someone else moving in unbeknownst to you.

When setting the expectations, let the tenant(s) know that if they leave the property in good, clean condition, you won't pursue any damages beyond the typical wear and tear of the property. If the property is left in good, clean condition, you have a certain amount of time in which you need to document any damages and return the security deposit to the tenant. This timeline is different from one area to the next, so check the laws of your locality to learn what your timeline is. Many localities set it at 30 days, but some have a shorter timeline.

If there are any damages that you will be withholding security deposit funds to cover, you need to document these with time-stamped pictures and descriptions. Doing this as quickly as possible will help your case since no one can accuse you of having other people in the house who damaged the property after the tenant left.

If, for some reason, you need to evict someone, you will need to contact your attorney, post a time-dated 3-day notice immediately, and begin the filing process. The attorney will take it from there. Then you need to wait for move-out in order to secure the property.

The important thing is to secure your property and get it cleaned up so that you can use your intake system to get a tenant who meets your standards. Once the old tenant is out and you have the information you need to send them any amount of the security deposit due them, begin with Steps 1 and 2, which deal with renovating your vacant property. After the renovations are completed, you will be ready to make the property the asset it should be!

**Holding a Note.** When you own a note, your job is to receive checks or wires each month until the debt has been satisfied. If you haven't already, contact your borrower to set up a system so that they can pay you each month on time. Regardless of whether they pay by check or electronically, you need to record these payments using some sort of software, just as you do rent checks. If the payments include interest, it's important to keep track of the interest paid and to create an amortization schedule. You will also need to send them a tax form in January each year with the amount of interest paid because they are able to use that as a tax write-off. You must supply this for them. The best way to do this is have a system in place at the outset or use prepaid software that is designed for this. You can also use a third-party servicing company to handle all of this for you at an affordable rate. The payment will go to the third-party servicing company, and then they will send you the payment after recording everything. You can keep it this simple! Remember, if you are holding only one note, it is simple to keep track of yourself. If you have 50, it becomes a little more hectic, doesn't it? Be prepared.

---

**GREAT QUESTION: AM I PROCEEDING IN A SYSTEMATIC WAY TO SECURE MY PROPERTIES AND EXPAND MY BUSINESS?**

---

## STEP SIX
# Building an Intake System for the Business

At this point you have secured leads, solved problems for multiple people, and now own property that you can hold, rent out, and build wealth. Congratulations! Unfortunately, you won't make a dime if you don't have an organized intake system for your business. You may inherit problematic tenants, or you may own a vacant property that needs work so that it will begin producing income for you every month. If you have failed to establish your own systematic guide to follow, you will likely repeat the problems of the previous owner and suffer a similar fate, constantly having to rehab property and remove problematic tenants. This process becomes endlessly frustrating, stressful, and expensive. You will hear people talk about real estate as if it is the worst possible investment on the planet. These are the people who failed to understand the business side of renting property and ended up with a revolving door of problems and damages. Let's talk about how to avoid this so that you can build a free-flowing business that helps you grow instead of having to start from scratch every few months.

I want you to think about your personal residence right now. This may sound odd, but think about the quality of your home right now. Is it nice? Is it dirty? Is it updated? Does it have upgraded mechanicals? Is it problematic? Has the property been a pleasure to be in?

Think about how your property currently makes you feel. Does it bring you peace? Does it make you cringe? Are you constantly worried and stressed?

Do you want to move? Would you be okay staying where you are? Are you proud of your home, or ashamed? Do you think about moving often, or occasionally? When you come to your front door, does it make you smile, or does it motivate you to work harder? Does it bring you down emotionally?

There are no right and wrong answers to the above questions, but I want you to consider how these feelings could affect your rental portfolio. I bet if your home is updated, clean, and has minimal maintenance, you are motivated to take care of it and keep it well-maintained. I would also bet that you feel a certain level of pride in your property, whether you are renting it or own it, and that it allows you to rest easy and incentivizes you keep it that way. A quality living space that is well-kept, clean, updated, and in line with your financial standing WILL motivate you to keep the property nice. THIS IS WHAT WE WANT TO PROVIDE!

On the other end of the spectrum is property that is run-down and dangerous, with deferred maintenance, and financially problematic to a tenant. How do you think this makes someone feel? The tenant has no pride in the property. He or she doesn't care whether the property is well-kept because the owner has no pride in it. The tenant follows suit and allows the property to become damaged and dirty. This eventually snowballs and affects the emotions and feelings of the tenant, who will eventually become like his or her surroundings--problematic. This will result in constant maintenance issues, large expenses, serial problematic tenants, and the constant need to rehab property when someone moves out. Does this sound like something you want to be dealing with day in and day out? Does this sound like wealth building? I don't think so.

When building an intake system for your business, you need to represent yourself and your business. This means that if you feel negative about some aspect of a property, someone else will, too! Take the time to fix small issues and do necessary updates so that you have the ability to build a good relationship and earn a long-term customer for your business. Long-term tenants and minimal maintenance are what builds wealth, given some time. My goal is always to have the nicest rental property in the area so that all of my tenants have pride in where they live and, in turn, take care of the property. All too often I see people skip a $150 fix because they see it as an expense. Later, it ends up costing them thousands, due to unhappy tenants who leave. Remember, we are in a service business!

So, what are the steps for building an intake for our business, beyond taking care of others and providing quality property to make people appreciative of their home? There are some key factors we need to keep in mind when renting out a property. Let's cover a few now.

1. You need to understand who is renting your property. You need to abide with any laws and regulations so that you don't discriminate against anyone since this is illegal, but you also want to protect your investment as best as possible and place only the best possible tenants.

2. Rental applications are vital. Design an application that enables you to check out the tenant and get an idea of how he or she will fit into your business. Collect the personal contact information of possible tenants and explain the rules of the property to them. This application should also clearly state who will be renting the property and require disclosures and an authorization for background checks. There should also be a small fee for filing the rental application. This will automatically help filter out people who aren't serious and those who don't want their backgrounds investigated for some reason. This is key for establishing a desired culture in your property.

3. Background and credit checks follow the initial application. It is important to run these as they will indicate whether a possible tenant pays his bills, has a criminal history, or is someone who would be a perfect tenant for you while he or she continues to build his/her lives. What we typically look for is someone with no evictions and someone who has minimal credit report issues. It is okay for people to have credit problems since this is usually why they are renting and not buying, but you want to look for someone who might have a lower score, but good habits. What does this mean? This means someone who goes to work, pays his or her bills, but maybe doesn't pay his or her student loans. This is an example of someone who may be a good person and a good renter, but who doesn't make enough

to pay the student loans. This is a person who is a "700" credit score person, with an actual score of 540. You want to keep an eye out for these opportunities and not pass them by.

If you find someone who is riddled with evictions, a poor credit score, and a criminal history, then you know you need to pass on that person because he/she doesn't fit your minimum requirements for a renter. A great question to ask when filling out the paperwork is, "Is there anything that I should expect to see on these reports?"

This question will give the applicant a chance to open up about any possible previous issues because he or she believes it will be revealed when you do the checking. Many times, they will even tell you about situations or issues that won't pop up on a background check. This is what you want. You will get a feel for their honesty, their past, and their possible future. That one simple question will generate answers that create context as well. We have had situations in which someone's background check showed a specific crime that, without context, would have eliminated that person from being able to rent from us. However, when asked prior to the check, the applicant explained what had happened, and we allowed the process to move forward because of it. Don't forget to ask great questions!

4. You now know the mindset for creating great experiences and property. You have a rental application. You understand how to maneuver the background and credit checks. Now you need to understand the leasing process.

You want a strict, but fair, lease. We don't allow a tenant to lease for less than one year initially. This helps create longer-term relationships and minimize turnover. Remember, vacancy is a huge expense. The lease needs to be signed by anyone over the age of 18 who will be moving into the property and by the property manager/owner. At the time the lease is signed, the manager needs to collect a security deposit. The security deposit should be equal to one month's rent. The first month's rent also needs to be collected at this time. Do not sway on this. These are your requirements for renters, and they will also serve to eliminate people who aren't serious about staying and taking care of the property.

When you create these extra hoops that a potential tenant must jump through, you are constantly refining the field of quality tenants from which to pick. This is important for the long-run sustainability of your business. It may be scary at first, but you will thank yourself for being so strict as time goes by because your business will run smoother and grow larger with less maintenance.

5. After the lease has been signed, the manager should walk the property with the newly-signed tenant and explain any specific rules not already discussed. The manager should have a checklist to use during the walk through. The tenant will have the opportunity to note any possible issues with the property, and the manager can use the checklist to mark down any damages or cleaning issues that might have been overlooked. This is so that the tenant doesn't get charged for something that he or she didn't do when the time comes for the tenant to move out. Understanding and documenting the exact condition of the property prevents future problems.

At the conclusion of the walkthrough, both the manager and the tenant need to sign the checklist, indicating that they understand the current contents and condition of the property. This checklist will also create smoother move-ins since you will be reminded of anything that might be missing, such as an appliance or utility.

Lastly, the manager should provide contact information so that the tenant can call with further questions or to talk to management. We have designed a contact sheet with an FAQ sheet so that tenants understand what number to call with general issues, the emergency number, what constitutes as an emergency, and what items they should or shouldn't call about. Setting this expectation is essential! If you don't establish firm standards regarding what items constitute a legitimate reason to call and what items don't, you will quickly discover that some tenants believe you to be a maid service, which isn't the case. Make sure you set standards.

Example:

Use the emergency line to report running water that you can't stop.

Do not call if you see a bug in the house.

6. At this point your tenant is ready to move in. The individual has passed your vetting system. You have accepted this person into your business. The tenant understands how much the rent is and where to send it. He or she understands any penalties or late fees associated with past-due payments and what to call about and what to handle him/herself. The tenant and management team now have a full understanding of each other and know exactly what to expect from one another. This is setting up your business for big success! Keep this going.

One of the most dangerous things that can happen in your business is to place a tenant without using an intake system similar to the one described above and make money off of them. This will create a bad habit and solidify a false sense of security and growth. This will enable problems to increase, and once the unorganized system does begin to fall, it will become exponentially more difficult to save. I learned this when I was a full-time day trader before I moved into real estate full time. If I made money on a bad trade, it solidified a bad practice. This sets you up to be burnt badly on down the road. If you are someone who currently has no intake system, but has a few properties generating money, be very cautious moving forward and begin implementing new strategies immediately.

**GREAT QUESTION: IS THERE ANYTHING I SHOULD EXPECT TO SEE ON THIS BACKGROUND CHECK?**

## STEP SIX
# Your First Check and How to Expect to Feel

You should be feeling proud at this point! You have taken the steps to shift your mind from collecting lump sums of cash to building streams of income that will set you free financially. Now you have just received your first rent check, or a monthly payment on a note! How do you feel? How should you feel?

When your first check comes in, the red carpet rolls out, and champagne falls from the heavens. You will feel elated, and you should! You just took a step that most of the entire population of the earth hasn't been able to take. Remember what we talked about earlier? Doing the opposite of what most others are doing will create a better life for us, and you just succeeded!

The first payment you receive will make this entire process real for you. You will understand what to expect and how to continue refining your business. The first check shifts the mind from desire to fruition, which allows you to move towards your next deal and next line of income quicker and more efficiently. Congratulations!

Expect your mind to move now to a new exciting and inspired phase in which you begin asking yourself how you can repeat this process and create even more. As you begin to comprehend fully what it means to earn income repeatedly and passively, you can expect to begin running numbers and constructing timelines for creating exactly what you want because you will be feeling the joy of earning income without trading time for it.

Don't forget to celebrate this victory, though!

---

**GREAT QUESTION: AM I ALLOWING MYSELF TO BE EXCITED FOR COMPLETING SUCH A HUGE MILESTONE?**

---

# STEP SIX
# How to Get it Again

The first check came in, and we feel great! We love real estate! So, how do we get this again? This is usually about the time that people try to reinvent the wheel and modify what they are doing that worked so well before and got them their first or second rental property. Don't do this!

After you have your first property under your belt, I want you to examine the process that you used to acquire that property. Look at the lead generation. Look at the key factors that contributed to your closing on the property. Look at the type of problem that you solved. Consider the details of the property and the type of tenant you have now. Think of the process you followed to create the new line of repeat income. Evaluate the business model you used with the intake and the management of the property.

When you evaluate the entire situation at hand, you will see that what you are doing is now repeatable and scalable. The lessons taught in this book thus far were all targeted to how to scale your business without having to scale your time investment, or even your operations. This is how businesses can hit scale. This is how you are going to get more property. You want to follow the exact process that you used on your first property.

Use the same marketing techniques. Target the same problem and provide a similar solution. This will make you the go-to resource in the area for these types of problems, and pretty soon you will see your business expand as your reputation grows. Work with the same types of properties in similar areas. You and your team now understand how to solve these types of problems and make these types of properties profitable. Do what works, and do what is proven! There is no need to branch out at this point to work with different types of people, businesses, or property types. Slow down and perfect your business. Remember, you don't need to make a million dollars today to change your life.

There is no secret to getting your second, third, or fourth property. Repeat the processes that are working for you and your specific market. You will feel like you need to be doing more, but, in reality, you don't! This is why we chose the path of creating repeated cashflow. We don't need to do more every time. If this were the case, we wouldn't be free, would we?

## GREAT QUESTION: AM I REPEATING WHAT WORKED FOR ME THE FIRST TIME?

# STEP SIX
# WHAT TO EXPECT WHEN SCALING

As previously mentioned, the steps you have been learning are founded on being able to scale and grow so that you become more and more financially free over time instead of inundated with more and more problems that take more and more of your personal time. That being said, businesses have problems, and businesses have downtimes during which it feels uncomfortable, like the investments required are never-ending. This is okay! This can be a sign that you are actually doing things correctly. Don't be afraid of a little pain. Remember, pain brings comfort later on.

### Winter is Coming!

At some point, winter will hit your business. It is impossible to avoid this, so it is best to expect it and protect yourself from it. It could be the result of market shifts. It could be a bump in vacancy across multiple properties at once due to the season of the year and tenants' deciding to move out, even though you have provided a great service and property. It could be an increase in maintenance needs or weather creating problems during a bad season. These things happen. It's okay. These things won't put you out of business. They will make your life uncomfortable for a short amount of time, and you will be better prepared for the future because of it. Embrace these times and be proud when you work through them.

Weathering the storm is part of business. How can we do it better each time? We learn! During tough times, we listen; we watch; and we evaluate everything that we do. When we experience these trying times, we learn how to grow and scale more efficiently and effectively.

We will learn how much liquidity we need at any given time. We will learn where our weak links in the business lie and where we need to reinforce our foundation. Be grateful for these times! They will only make you stronger.

Now, in addition to expecting to have the typical struggles of business and some tough times that must be endured, you can expect the benefits of scale! You can expect the ability to provide more resources for your business. You can expect to see changes in the options and time available to you and your family. You can expect to see changes in your mindset and outlook on life as you have the ability to look at more opportunity.

One beautiful aspect of scale is that it allows you to provide opportunity and income to more and more people. You can provide more work for skilled laborers. You provide security for employees and partners. With new partners, you create the opportunity to work on larger and larger projects as they become available. You will surpass established milestones and have the ability to set new ones.

You will learn to take care of your personal needs and also realize that growing the business is more beneficial than your singular personal needs. This allows you to scale even larger in mind, body, and finance.

You will see one deal turn into 3, and 3 into 5, and 5 into 15. You will begin finding joy in refining your systems and business so that you can better provide for everyone around you. This is the difference between running a business and owning a job. Remember, anyone who owns a job is primarily focused on taking care of himself and possibly those closest to him. The business owner is focused on taking care of everyone--customers, family, friends, employees, employees' families, and future generations alike.

Our purpose is to scale. Wealth is measured in time. Scale will allow our wealth to cover future generations instead of just the current one.

---

## GREAT QUESTION: IS MY PRIMARY FOCUS TO TAKE CARE OF EVERYONE, OR JUST MYSELF?

---

# STEP SIX
# UNDERSTANDING ASSET CLASSES

Understanding what you and your partners are investing in is important. Below I discuss some common principles that you can work into your business and your investing identity. Be aware of the type of asset class with which you are working. There are different "grades" of asset classes within real estate. Each grade brings different benefits and problems with them. Once you understand which asset class fits your identity the best, you can target it for acquisitions and investments.

**"A Class"** – These properties are in top-tier locations with high-end price tags. These properties typically generate less monthly cashflow than other asset classes, but offer the most opportunity for appreciation and large payouts upon sale. These assets typically have higher-end tenants as well because the rental rates on these properties are much higher than rates in the other classes. "A Class" properties also have endless lending opportunities. Since they are the nicest real estate available, lender money is typically well protected. A downside to these properties is that when the market shifts downward, the Class A tenants move to Class B properties. This can create vacancy issues while you still continue having to soak up high purchase prices and holding costs.

**"B Class"** – Below "A Class" properties in location and purchase price, but still properties with the possibility of some appreciation and good lending options. This is a personal favorite class of mine since "B Class" properties can provide great cashflow, appreciate, and attract top-tier tenants, even in a down market. The downside to "B Class" properties is the lack of potential appreciation opportunity when compared to "A Class" property. Additionally, rental rates may not be the top possible rate. Nevertheless, because of the lower purchase price, these properties still typically produce better monthly cashflow than "A Class" properties that have been financed with debt.

**"C Class"** – Entering a "C Class" location will provide a unique opportunity. Many "C Class" properties will provide the best possible monthly cashflow since purchase prices are well below the top two asset classes. The tradeoff is that the business must be able to withstand the more common issues these types of properties present. "C Class" properties have very little, if any, opportunity for appreciation, so you need to understand how to buy these properties in a manner that ensures you have equity upon purchase. These properties can be more difficult to sell to retail buyers and may take longer to rent to a tenant who can pass your qualifications. There will also be minimal lending opportunities from traditional sources, such as banks, because these properties don't meet their lending requirements. These properties may be in neighborhoods with some drug and crime issues, but the nice part is that there will always be pockets of nicer, cleaner "C Class" homes, where the area is very blue collar, in which you can invest. These areas make for great investment opportunities, giving you cashflow month to month while you build a reputation for serving in the community. These areas are lower income, but not on the poverty line. "C Class" properties can be great in down markets as well because renters in the "A" and "B" classes will then be looking for safe properties with lower rental rates.

**"D Class"** – These properties are crippled with crime and drug problems. These are high renter areas with very low ownership rates. The purchase prices of these homes don't allow for borrowing and are much riskier for personal investing. If looking to invest in areas like this, you can expect virtually no opportunity for appreciation without a major overhaul to the culture in the area. You can also expect maintenance issues and tenant problems. Investing in these areas becomes very relational as well. These assets will have lower rental rates and purchase prices. Having an organized team is essential for investing in any class below "C Class." Government assistance and payment help is common with this class.

**"F Class"** – This area is commonly called a "warzone." These zones are communities in which major issues exist with the actual structure of the area. These could range from water and sanitation issues to extreme crime and drug trafficking. These areas also commonly have large vacancy and abandonment issues due to underfunding and loss of major industry in the area that previously supported the economy. Major lenders typically steer away from these properties.

Now that you understand the different asset classes and the difference in how you would operate within them, you can choose the one that may fit you and your team best. When choosing a class to focus on, it is important to understand that leveraging the upside within that class will bring the greatest benefit. As an example, you never want to focus on appreciation within the "C Class" because appreciation will be minimal, if there is any whatsoever. Instead you want to focus on monthly cashflow and the possibility of creating sizeable monthly income with minimal capital investment due to the fact that the purchase prices are lower than those in the "A" and "B" classes. Always double down on the upside of the class instead of attempting to diversify within the class. If you buy right in the "C Class," is there an opportunity to grow your equity? Of course! But, should you count on it? Never.

## GREAT QUESTION: WHICH ASSET CLASS BEST FITS MY IDENTITY?

## BONUS STEP
# WHAT IF YOU FOCUS ON PROBLEMS WITH MUCH LARGER PROPERTIES ATTACHED TO THEM?

What if you were to apply all of the principles and practices in this book to properties that are much larger? When most people think of purchasing a property at a discount, wholesaling a house, or building a portfolio, their minds tend to shift to lower-end properties for whatever reason. It is easier to think of a lower-class neighborhood having more problems than an "A Class" neighborhood, but, at the end of the day, there are problems everywhere.

I want you to understand that when you locate problems and stack enough of them together, the size of the property doesn't matter. The process is still the same, whether it's a 700 square-foot house worth $20,000 or a 6,000 square-foot house worth $1,000,0000. The only thing that changes with these properties is the size of the spread you can create, and the potential for larger profits.

When problems exist, the larger and more expensive properties cause even more stress than the smaller, more affordable ones. Larger properties have a smaller buyer pool and have less chance of selling quickly in many cases. This is where you have the opportunity to problem-solve for people and negotiate much larger deals, with much more profit built in, but no more work than a smaller, cheaper property requires.

Don't be afraid to market to these larger properties as well. These people are often under-served because investors pass them by as "never having problems" when, in reality, they are people with the same exact problems as everyone else. I have a perfect example of how to stack problems to solve when dealing with sellers of larger-than-normal properties. This is another of my personal experiences.

When marketing to possible sellers, I always make sure to focus a piece of my marketing on trusts and LLCs. Many people don't realize that a lot of LLCs are sole-owner structures. This means that the person who makes the decision to sell is the only one involved in the transaction. It also means that any property held by that LLC is more likely to experience problems if that sole owner has some sort of financial or personal trouble. When these people have problems, they typically have no one to turn to because no one has reached out to help them at any point.

I received a call from an LLC owner who had a portfolio of properties in a trust. I was the only one who ever mailed marketing materials to him, and he contacted me because the letter had been handwritten. We talked for a bit, and I learned he wanted to shed his responsibility for the properties and set his beneficiary up for success after he was gone. In this case, his wife was the beneficiary he wanted to protect. My single letter, which took mere seconds to compose, created a possible deal involving 20 different properties with creative financing options that I could evaluate, using the system I discussed earlier, to determine what type of offer would best solve the problem for the seller and still produce the best possible profit for my business. Let me tell you, closing on a portfolio of properties is much more exciting and beneficial than closing on just one. You will remember the feeling of closing on more than 15 properties at the same time forever!

This isn't limited to single-family properties, either. I have worked on 80-plus unit apartment complexes with sellers who have income and tax issues. I have worked on commercial buildings and storefronts. If a seller owns real estate, you can apply the principles in this book, regardless of what kind of real estate it is. I have friends and colleagues who own hundreds of units, and even thousands of units, obtained using the principles in this book. Once you master the art of designing solutions for problems, your potential is unlimited. The property no longer matters; your ability to ease people's pain becomes your biggest asset.

**GREAT QUESTION: IS MY MIND OPEN TO HELPING EVERYONE, AND NOT JUST A SELECT FEW PRECONCEIVED SELLER TYPES?**

# Can I Receive Bulk Payments and Passive Payments from the Same Deal?

If you had the ability and knowledge to structure a deal so that you could receive a bulk payment upfront while still receiving equity or passive payments on the backend, would you do it? Yes? Well good, because we are going to cover the concept now.

There are a number of ways in which you can receive multiple payments on a single property. You may not even own the property at any point and still receive not only a bulk payment upfront, but a monthly payment for a set amount of time as well. This can be done by selling either the property or your interest in a property creatively.

When you hold a controlling interest in a property, such as a lease-option, or a purchase agreement and assign it, you have the ability to structure the sale any way that best fits the transaction. If you have a larger spread, you can create a sale in which you are owed a "down payment" of sorts, with monthly payments on the backend.

As an example, assume you hold a controlling interest in a property, and the difference between the amount for which you can sell your interest and the amount you owe (i.e., your spread) is $50,000. You can structure a deal such that you receive $20,000 down, which you can reinvest in another asset, and receive the remaining $30,000 via a series of payments over time. This gives you cash upfront so that you can capitalize on more opportunities as well as backend cashflow on which you can build a consistent income stream. At the same time, the $30,000 remaining balance owed to you becomes an asset that you can sell if you wish at a later date. This type of thinking is what will help create multiple different angles and options in your business.

The best part about the above example is that it doesn't matter if you own the property, hold an interest in a purchase agreement on the property, or are holding an option to purchase it with a lease in place. You have the ability to negotiate and structure a sale on the backend that best fits your business for the season that it is in.

The final thing I want to mention in this section is that you can create these sales with multiple properties or packages simultaneously. You don't need to own the properties, and you can even complete this type of transaction while selling the company as a whole versus selling individual properties.

Yes, you can sell a company creatively as well. There are a multitude of ways in which you can do this, regardless of whether you want to create a simple contract for the sale of equity or create shares to sell over time. You can sell your ownership in a company creatively. You can even "wholesale" a company and receive payments, depending on what you negotiate.

I once was involved in a company that owned multiple properties, and it was decided that it was time to sell. My role was to locate a buyer for the properties. Originally this plan seemed like the best route. Sell each property individually or as a package so buyers could pick and choose. The problem was that this was heavy on resources and strenuous on multiple different buyers. The other issue was that selling outright was going to trigger some capital gains taxes, and we would also want to invest the proceeds from the sale into other assets. It was decided that selling on terms would be best. To best accomplish this, we decided to sell the company as a whole over time to someone who wanted to buy equity over time. This is essentially seller-financing the sale, but the seller has more responsibility (and incentive) to keep the company moving forward since the seller would still have the majority of the equity in the beginning. With the passage of time, the buyer purchases more and more equity until the seller is bought out, and the buyer owns the company outright.

This worked out for a number of reasons. The buyer had the security of knowing he was buying into a proven system that was already in place, and his wants matched perfectly with ours. Both parties would initially be working together to make the company as profitable as possible. This was true regarding both the real estate holdings and other product/service components. This was a way for the buyer to transition into the company and leverage what was working best. He could date the business before marrying it!

You may be wondering how in the world this gets structured. Believe it or not, this required only a two-page agreement that was drawn up by the seller's attorney. That's it. Since the buyer was purchasing equity in a business, there was no title or paper transfer of the properties themselves. The seller was being paid over a set number of months as the buyer created more and more equity for himself, and I was paid per the agreement.

Now that your wheels are turning, what if you were to connect the dots on a larger business, or multiple smaller packages under the same business entity? What if you checked with the laws and regulations in your market regarding brokering businesses or transactions such as this? (Not all states require licenses for brokering business transactions.) What if, in addition to property, you had the experience and ability to put large deals together without ever investing in them yourself and get paid hundreds of thousands of dollars over time for your efforts? The possibilities are limitless!

---

**GREAT QUESTION: AM I KEEPING AN OPEN MIND TO RECEIVING MULTIPLE TYPES OF PAYMENTS IN A SINGLE TRANSACTION BY CREATING DEALS THAT WORK WELL FOR MULTIPLE PARTIES?**

---

# Advantages of Leveraging Other Teams

Let me quickly touch on this creative advantage that too many people overlook in their business. When your business is fairly new and you want to scale, a great way to do so is by emulating and duplicating other businesses already doing what you want to be doing!

You have the ability to network and plug yourself into someone else's system and business without being invited. If you want to get involved in large multifamily property deals and buy apartment complexes, should you wing it and just start mailing complexes, or should you network with other owners first? You should locate other owners first! In networking with them, you will gain knowledge and experience, but, more importantly, you will learn what they want. When you find out what they buy--the types of properties that fit their criteria--go find those properties.

Now, here is the best part. You aren't going to wholesale a property to them or even make an offer on their behalf. You are going to pass the lead onto them after doing some due diligence. Doing the due diligence provides them with a well-founded lead. Whether the lead is ultimately good or bad is up to them to decide, but when you bring this lead to them, you will have the ability to be there every step of the way because you provided the lead. You are now the front-end link for the deal. You have the ability to speak to the seller. You have the ability to speak with the investors. You have the ability to be there on inspection day if the buyer feels the numbers or property is decent enough to consider. This will gain you firsthand experience, and it isn't uncommon for you to get some equity if the deal comes to fruition.

You basically became an acquisitions manager in order to learn firsthand from someone doing what you want to do. At the same time, you produced value for a future partner.

This action will offer you endless opportunities. Too many fail to consider this possibility because of a scarcity mentality and a fear of rejection. Create endless value for a possible long-term partner, and you will benefit long term as well. This can be done with any type of property, and even with other businesses. Inject yourself into their business culture and environment and work for free. Trust me when I say NO ONE else will be doing this. You will win big in the end. When you meet someone new and realize they need something that you can accomplish, do it. Provide it. Grow from it.

**GREAT QUESTION: AM I LISTENING TO WHAT OTHERS NEED SO THAT I CAN HELP PROVIDE THAT FREE OF CHARGE TO HELP CREATE BETTER LONG-TERM RELATIONSHIPS?**

# How to Obtain Equity in a Deal You Never Saw

Obtaining equity in a property can be done through purchasing, selling, locating, investing, or even by negotiating on behalf of the buyer. There are investors who specialize in negotiating deals for other investors, and they get paid by taking either a small amount of equity in the deals or a percentage of the sales price. There are others who get paid for raising and managing funds as well, although this involves much more red tape and working within the regulations of the Securities Exchange Commission (SEC). Always consult an attorney before attempting to raise funds to ensure you will be doing it legally and ethically.

Once you realize that you can earn equity by creating value in transactions, you open yourself up to doing so by providing whatever type of value you decide to deliver for each transaction. If you invest your own funds and resources into a deal along with another purchaser-investor, and you lend them funds, you will own the paper on a property, or you have the ability to take ownership in the property with them. It is all whatever works best for each party. "Life is a negotiation." A fellow investor and someone I admire taught me that.

You can also obtain an equity position by locating property for other investors. Instead of asking that your wholesale or assignment fee be paid as a lump sum or a series of monthly payments, you can ask for an equity stake so that if and when the property sells, you have the ability either to profit big on the backend or earn monthly payments.

Anytime you create value in someone's business, be aware that you may be able to take a small amount of equity as payment. When you open your mind to this, you open the possibility of it happening more and more. Simply talk to the closing agent or attorney to structure the paperwork in a way that makes the most sense for everyone. Whether you are creating a separate entity with an operating agreement or simply taking a small equity position in an existing entity is up to you and your partners.

---

**GREAT QUESTION: HOW CAN I ACQUIRE EQUITY IN MY NEXT DEAL BY CREATING VALUE IN SOMEONE ELSE'S BUSINESS?**

---

# You Can Do This on More Than Just Houses

An overwhelming theme for creating cashflow and financial freedom is having an open mind and looking at different problems from multiple perspectives before deciding on one that will work best for you and your future. A security position and repeat income when selling something is not specific to the sale of houses. You can create security and cashflow when the deal involves mobile homes, vehicles, land, and businesses alike.

We discussed how to create revenue by working with packages of properties held by a single business entity in the previous section. But what if someone is having a problem involving personal property, such as a mobile home? What if someone has a car he needs to sell, or you have some other kind of opportunity to purchase a vehicle for less than its true value?

Keeping your mind open to the possibility of creating repeat income in simple transactions such as these is key to crafting a life of financial freedom because these are quick and simple opportunities on which you have the ability to capitalize.

Mobile homes are perfect examples of this. When someone is selling a mobile home and the land is not included in the sale, the mobile home actually has a simple title similar to a car title. These transactions can be executed on the same day. There is no 30-day due diligence period during which title and land searches are completed by a title company.

The key to executing a simple transaction involving a mobile home or a car to generate repeat income is holding a secured position. When you become the bank on a car or mobile home title, you will be holding the clear title, while the buyer holds a memorandum title. This is identical to the situation wherein a dealership sells a vehicle to a buyer and finances the purchase. The dealership, or its financial subsidiary, will hold the clear title until the loan has been satisfied. Once the loan has been satisfied, the seller signs over the clear title to the buyer, and the transaction is complete.

When you sell a vehicle creatively, you will complete a "sheet of security" at the title bureau or attorney's office. This legally provides you with a clear title to the vehicle being used to secure the loan. Without a clear title, the buyer cannot legally sell the vehicle until you are made whole.

The above is a simple example of how you can locate an item of personal property that is selling below market value and resell it to a new buyer at market price, thus creating a free line of income from it. The beautiful part about this is that you will usually receive more than market value for the item because you will be earning interest on the sale over time. In the case study that follows, I discuss how I got a mobile home for only $3,000 and turned it into $8,000 in less than a week.

---

**GREAT QUESTION: IF I HAVE THE ABILITY TO HOLD AN ASSET AS SECURITY, AM I CONSIDERING THE POSSIBILITY OF CREATING ANOTHER LINE OF INCOME FROM IT?**

---

# Mobile Home Case Study

When I look at mobile homes that I might be able to turn over to generate cashflow, I typically look for homes that I have the ability to sell on terms, with a down payment that is equal to or greater than my initial investment. I don't ever want to wait to recoup my investment from a mobile home buyer. If I have my capital invested, I want it secured by an asset that has the possibility of either producing cashflow for decades and/or appreciating in value.

Mobiles homes are depreciating assets. Their value deteriorates over time, just as the value of cars do. We don't want our capital invested in assets that move in the wrong direction! This being said, I personally don't want to own the mobile home and have the responsibility involved with it. I want to finance the sale. That's it. This is what an investment in mobile homes means to me and my team.

Following is a detailed, picture-perfect example of creating cashflow through a mobile home financing transaction. We found this particular mobile home in a Buy/Sell/Trade group post on Facebook. The seller was moving into a house a few hours away and had no more need for the mobile home. The home was located in a mobile home park that did not allow rentals. Only owner-occupied mobile homes were permitted. This played into our strategy perfectly and allowed someone to own a home for less than what it cost that person to rent in the local market.

**Mobile Home Asking Price- $3,500**

**Purchase Price - $3,000**

## Mobile Home sold 72 hours after purchase

### Sale $3,500 down

### $200 per month for 24 months

### Profit: $5,300

The seller was willing to come down a few hundred dollars if the sale could be completed that day. I agreed, and we met at the title bureau, where a quick title search and transfer was completed. The process took only a few minutes, and the sale was finalized. After purchasing the property for $3,000, I posted a "for sale by owner" notice on the same Buy/Sell/Trade group Facebook page on which I had found the mobile home. I posted higher-quality photos, with a better sales ad, which included the benefits of the property and the availability of owner-financing that allowed for monthly payments.

The ad indicated a required down payment of $3,500 and monthly payment options of either $300 per month for 12 months or $200 per month for 24 months. The mobile home alone was worth somewhere in the neighborhood of $5,000. The park in which it was located had a couple other trailers for sale for around $5,000 that were in much worse condition. This created a real value for my trailer because it was move-in ready for less out-of-pocket than the others available nearby.

Within 72 hours I had multiple interested buyers and multiple walkthroughs. The mobile home ended up selling for $3,500 down, with payments of $200 per month for 24 months. I was officially cashed out when I received the down payment—and I earned a $500 profit to boot. The home was producing cashflow for me within 72 hours of purchase and paid me for the next 24 months consistently. I was effectively able to create a $5,300 profit on a simple $3,000 investment. This is a profit of well over 100%.

The benefits of structuring the deal in this fashion instead of owning the home and renting it out were that I had no tax responsibilities on the home, no mobile park lot rent, no utility payments, and no maintenance. I had a net gain of $5,300 with zero work involved beyond purchasing the home and listing it for sale. The mobile home served as security for the loan I had made, and, honestly, even if the buyer had picked up and moved the trailer to avoid paying, I had no financial risk whatsoever since I had received the full amount of my cash investment with the down payment. I also didn't have to worry about insurance or park rule changes. This was a win-win deal the moment it was sold. The buyer was able to pay an amount he could comfortably afford, and I had a new line of income each month. Not a bad trade!

---

**GREAT QUESTION: HOW CAN I CREATE MONTHLY INCOME WHILE TRADING ZERO TIME FOR IT?**

---

# Closing Thoughts

You now have the knowledge and tools to begin building cashflow into your business and freedom into your life! Take the steps discussed in this book, apply them to your business, and evaluate how each is working for you. Leverage what works best for you and your team and focus on building the best business that you can!

Your next step is to take relentless action to shift your income from "earned" to "repeat." Let nothing stand in your way and recognize that the excuses you give yourself for why you can't complete this in the time frame that you desire are just that--excuses. Remember the struggles and difficulties that I shared with you. Remember that no matter where you are at today, it is only your starting point, and what you do from this point on is what will determine how far you get. Your day-to-day action is what will decide your future.

The world and the markets don't care about your circumstances. The world holds no grudges or bias against you. The market only cares about the value created and the effort exerted day to day. Notice I said "day to day." Consistency will forever be the catalyst for your change. There will be times when quitting will be easier. Use this as the signal to take a single step that day to continue your consistent movement forward. If the step feels like it might have been in reverse, I promise that it was still a necessary step that actually helped you move forward. The killer of all success is inaction and stagnancy.

Become obsessed with creating time-freedom and cashflow in your life and business. Each dollar you churn from "earned" to "repeat," is a small piece of freedom you gain. Before you realize it, you will be free, with the option to create the life that you wish with the people you wish. Start now and work on creating just one dollar per month. Practice the skills and mindset of delayed gratification and forever reap the rewards for looking toward the future instead of at what's for lunch today.

I thank you for your support in purchasing and reading this book. I wish nothing but massive success for you and your loved ones. I would love nothing more than to hear about your wins and stories from reading this book. You can share them with me on Instagram @Todd_M_Fleming

Have A Day!

## TODD M FLEMING

# Special Thanks

A very special thanks to my mentor and one of my closest friends, Ben Walkley. Ben, you have forever changed my life and the life of so many others by taking me under your wing and showing me the true, ethical, and transparent process of doing business and living life with fulfilment. Words cannot express the gratitude that I hold for you, and I thank God every day that He brought us together in the way that He did. You taught me the true purpose in real estate and problem solving. I often wonder where I would be in life if I hadn't had the pleasure of meeting you, and I truly believe that I would not be an author, successful investor, or educator. I thank you not only for your mentorship and friendship, but for being a great man, father, and husband. The example that you set in your daily actions creates an energy and atmosphere that I strive to achieve in my own life on a daily basis. You remind me that I am enough and that it's okay to strive for new greatness every day. Thank you for your constant love and support from the bottom of my heart.

P.S. I still don't want to go camping....

**Ben Is the founder and owner of Fireland Title Group in northeast Ohio as well as the Fireland School of Real Estate that teaches aspiring real estate investors and agents hands-on techniques for growing within real estate and building financial freedom.**

Thank you to my loving wife, Denise, and son, Wyatt. Thank you for pushing me every day to be the best me possible. Wyatt, you teach me more than I could ever teach you. You remind me what's truly important in life, and I wouldn't trade our "Wednesdays With Wyatt" for anything. Denise, thank you for your endless support and thought in creating the best possible family atmosphere and always wanting the best for our family. Thank you for reminding me where all of these blessings truly come from and how to be grateful. I can't fully express my gratitude to you for putting up with my late-night writing sessions and constant brainstorming on how to create the best life possible. I know it isn't always easy being with someone who always has 12 more ideas, with plans for how to launch them into reality. Your ability to understand operations and implementation has been a key component in making all of this possible. I love you.

Stop bringing home dogs, though… seriously.

**Denise and Todd were married in 2016, and Wyatt was born later that same year.**


Thank you to the Kingdom Real Estate family. You could never understand the love and pride I hold in being able to interact with over 1,000 of you. The support you have shown for the vision and movement of creating a community of investors moving forward to create a life of freedom and choice is truly incredible. I am sincerely humbled by everything that each and every member has been able to accomplish and share with others.

**Todd is the founder of TheKingdomRealEstate.com wherein a community of investors interact daily to achieve their wildest dreams through real estate.**


Thank you to my fellow investing partner and team member Dustin Lloyd. None of this is possible without your constant support and open mind in creating long-term wealth through real estate investing. I appreciate our conversations, and your friendship means the world to me. Your friendship has shown me what's possible in this life if you continue to focus on expanding and growing with consistency. Don't stop inspiring!

**Dustin is the founder and owner of KeySmartInc.com, which supplies automotive keys and accessories to the entire nation.**

Thank you to YOU! Thank you to you the reader. Thank you for choosing this book to move your business and life forward. The love and support shown for the "I've Got Nothing For You" series has been nothing short of incredible, and I thank you for making it a best seller. I could have never dreamed of being a successful author until you made it possible. I will forever be grateful for everything you have done, and I will endeavor to continue to share the best possible information and experiences so that you, the reader, can benefit and grow from it. I want nothing more than for you to become financially free. My purpose in life is to end financial suffering, and it starts with you! So, let's do it together!

Thank you, God, for the blessings and ability to write, learn, and experience new levels of life every day. Thank You for the health and wealth of my family and loved ones. None of this is possible without Your love. Thank You for introducing me to all the influential people in my life who share the same drive and love for living life as I do. Thank You for constantly showing me the best possible path for helping others and creating love.

# About the Author

Todd Fleming's purpose in life is to end financial suffering and create a world with financial stability. Todd has built his financial freedom through real estate holdings, which include both property and secured notes, as well as his educational companies, The Power of Finance and The Kingdom Real Estate. Todd currently spends his time every day with his wife Denise, son Wyatt, and two dogs, Gracie and Winston. He focuses daily on creating his ideal day and working towards a more impactful life.

Todd began his career in real estate by wholesaling property prior to transitioning to property ownership and note creation. Todd currently teaches financial principles and freedom through his companies, PowerOfFinance.com and TheKingdomRealEstate.com. Todd believes that financial freedom is a choice and a set of repeatable actions. His goal is to reach as many people as possible in order to change as many lives as possible.

In the future, Todd plans to create content for all ages, helping others avoid the pitfalls of early-adulthood financial mistakes and borrowing. Todd has upcoming children's books and courses to help people become financially stable and eliminate bad debt while creating extra savings and financial options previously misunderstood. This content will be found at PowerOfFinance.com.

You can follow Todd on Instagram @Todd_M_Fleming for daily free content, teachings, giveaways, and support!

# Want to Work with Todd?

If you are located in northeastern Ohio and want hands-on training, join www.Fireland.School to work with Ben Walkley and Todd Fleming together.

Work with Todd digitally at **www.TheKingdomRealEstate.com** for national and international training.

Work with Todd on financial principles and financial freedom at **www.PowerOfFinance.com** to unlock your finances, eliminate bad debt and create freedom.

# Recommended Media

**Five Book Recommendations by Todd:**

1. *Life and Work Principles* by Ray Dalio
2. *Disrupt You* By Jay Samit
3. *Man's Search For Meaning* by Viktor E. Frankl
4. *Start With Why* by Simon Sinek
5. *The Compound Effect* By Darren Hardy

**Social Media Channels to follow on Instagram:**

@Todd_M_Fleming

@SecretEntourage

@TheKingdomRealEstate

@PowerOfFinance

# Todd's Other Books

This Book is Part 2 of 3 in the "I've Got Nothing For You" series.

Book 1: *If You Can't Wholesale After This... I've Got Nothing For You*

Book 2: *If You Can't Cashflow After This... I've Got Nothing For You*

**Upcoming Books**

Children's Books, Financial Literacy Books, Book 3 in the "I've Got Nothing For You" series

Sign up to Todd's Newsletter at **www.ToddMFleming.com** to receive updates on all new releases and content!

# Acknowledgements and Testimonials

**Brandon Richards**

**Owner at Fearless Properties LLC and Host of the Fearless Pursuit of Freedom Podcast**

Cashflow is the bloodline of your business and life. Without it, you will never be able to set yourself, or your family free. This book is quite literally a step by step instructional guide on how to mold your mind to one of abundance, whilst learning to be a leader and innovator ON your new business rather than IN your business.

Learn the importance of a team, AND how to build it with a solid foundation. As well as what/who to look for and what questions to ask your prospective employees. Real estate can be a real beating, but in this book you learn how to dodge the left and right hooks while setting up your counter attack.

**Ashley Murphy**

**Owner/Designer at Fearless Properties LLC**

Todd opens up his own, transparent, real-life stories to encourage you to trust in yourself that this plan of yours to be financially free is absolutely achievable!

In real estate, things are going to go wrong. Todd outlines how with the right mindset and due diligence, there is a way to set yourself up for success instead of failure when things occasionally and inevitably do go very wrong.

This easy to read book engagingly suggests that you reevaluate your mindset when it comes to getting out of the rat race and bringing in cashflow! He genuinely helps you learn how you can improve your financial status for generations to come if you choose to take action.

Todd openly shares investment secrets with you that many other real estate experts will gladly charge you hundreds or even thousands of dollars for without hesitation. His ability and willingness to teach others to do what he does is truly admirable and honest.

**Sarah Weber**

**Owner of Rising Star Properties LLC**

Not only is Todd's book helpful because it is laid out step by step, but he breaks down every Real Estate related term he references to and goes into detail to explain them so people who are brand new to the industry can understand. It is so beginner friendly, you don't really find yourself having lingering questions like with many other books and resources.

He doesn't hide his emotions or struggles he instead uses them to further explain how to solve problems that pop up while in the process of completing deals. His relatability throughout the book makes it much more appealing as he doesn't portray himself as an all-knowing expert, but rather someone who started with little knowledge and is constantly learning and evolving his business by learning from his mistakes. It was extremely motivating to realize that I don't have to go into my business with perfect knowledge of how to do every little thing.

"If You Can't Cashflow After This" expanded my mind and thought process while giving me the confidence to take massive imperfect action with a laid out, step-by-step action plan!

**RJ Bates III**
Owner of Titanium Investments
Host of The Titanium Vault Podcast
Executive Director of Beat Kid's Cancer

Todd has an extraordinary talent in breaking down the intricacies of real estate investing into easy to understand and actionable steps. His delivery of explaining the importance of cash flow and how to truly create passive income is masterfully crafted. Regardless of your experience as an investor, this book gives quality advice on how to advance to the next level.

**Valerie Lloyd**
**Owner of KeySmart Inc**

This book is truly a life changer. 1) My husband and I read this together and were able to convert our "daily grind" business into a passive income business. We are now able to concentrate our time on finding more investments. 2) We have used the principles shared in this book to change our beliefs about investments. Growing up in a 401K, stocks and state retirement family, I never really thought about any real "backing" to investments. Those can all disappear in the blink of an eye. Real estate doesn't. And lastly 3) We have been able to turn our rental processes into real systems that make it easy and quick to handle any situation. Less time on business, less time on hassles and less financial stress equals more time for us to spend on what matters; family, friends, health and happiness.

**Dustin Lloyd**

**Owner of KeySmart Inc and Managing Member of Alcatraz Holdings Realty**

I have been lucky enough to have had Todd teach me some of the principles in this book and I have already put them into action. If you follow this guide it will put you, not only, on the path to financial freedom but to a much happier life.

CPSIA information can be obtained
at www.ICGtesting.com
Printed in the USA
BVHW081237110219
539956BV00017B/831/P